LUTHER'S
PRAYERS

LUTHER'S PRAYERS

Edited by
Herbert F. Brokering

Augsburg
MINNEAPOLIS

LUTHER'S PRAYERS

Library of Congress Cataloging-in-Publication Data

Luther, Martin, 1483-1546.
    [Selections. English. 1994]
    Luther's prayers / edited by Herb Brokering.
       p.   cm.
    Includes indexes.
    ISBN 0-8066-2755-7 (alk. paper)
    1. Lutheran Church — Prayer-books and devotions — English.
    2. Prayers.   I. Brokering, Herbert F.   II. Title.
BR331.E5   1994
242'.8041—dc20   94-24889
                                                       CIP

The paper used in this publication meets the minimum requirements of American National Standard for Information Sciences — Permanence of Paper for Printed Library Materials, ANSI Z329.48-1984.   ∞™

Manufactured in the United States of America   AF 9-2755

                                         6   7   8   9   10

CONTENTS

Preface
7

Preparation for Prayer
9

The Lord's Prayer
21

A Simple Way to Pray
39

Prayers for Enlightenment from God's Word
63

Prayers for a Christian Life
81

Prayers When Death Draws Near
99

Indexes
109
A. The Catechism
B. Home and Family
C. Word and Sacraments
D. Church

Preface

There is no monotony in the prayer salutations of Luther. Some are lengthy. He is as one in continual conversation with God. To him the name of God is the presence of God. Many of the prayers end as abruptly as they begin. Some close with several *Amens*, like a hallelujah chorus.

The prayers show Luther as one deeply dependent upon grace and mercy. Mercy, mercy, was his plea, and he trusted that mercy was always present in Christ. Mercy was Luther's plea. Mercy was God's promise.

It is clear that his faith and confession became devotion and prayer. The chief parts of the *Small Catechism*, so well known as statements of faith, as seen here, are natural avenues of prayer for Luther. His interpretation was rooted and strengthened and nourished in prayer. Doctrine was his way of life. It was the topic for each of his prayers. A credal statement was always in need of meditation and devotion. It was no end in itself.

Grace had meaning to him in his daily living. He was not a man to go recklessly into the presence of God, but he went boldly. He went as one absolutely forgiven.

One has the impression that Luther was more conversational than editorial in his prayers. He was not praying for a printer. Some of the prayers resemble devotional extractions or devotional starters. They open thoughts for meditation. They are the quick and sometimes quiet blurting out or whispering of a deeply dependent creature.

Words that have become clichés to some are critical words in the life of this man. He uses the language of faith with force and abandonment. He leans into these words with meaning.

The prayers are on topics spanning all of life. The soldier, employer, politician, pastor, sick person, parent, newlywed, teacher.

One might wish to retain in these translations the rhythm and meter and mental images of this 16th century Saxon preacher and poet. It may be that the prayers find some of their poetry in this day as they are prayed aloud.

Herbert F. Brokering

PREPARATION FOR PRAYER

My God, you will not abandon my
hope. You will hear my prayer
and satisfy my desires. I will pray
and wait for your grace. Hear
me and fulfill my hope.

PREPARATION FOR PRAYER

1.

For the Removal of Sins

Lord, it is your will and command that we should come to you and pray. So I now come to please you. I ask you to forgive and to remove my sins which weigh heavily upon me. Let them not prevent me from coming to you in prayer. Amen.

2.

For Help to Overcome Sense of Unworthiness

Lord, it is for your honor and to your service that I now ask. Oh be praised and glorified. I plead, fully aware that you have glory, and that I am a poor, undeserving sinner. I cannot be without your help. You are willing and able to grant it to all who ask for it. Oh see my need and misery, and help me for your honor's sake. Amen.

3.

Praise for Christ's Love

Oh gracious God, I am fully aware that I am unworthy. I deserve to be a brother of Satan and not of Christ. But Christ, your dear Son, died and rose for me. I am his brother. He earnestly desires that I should believe him, without doubt and fear. I need no longer regard myself as unworthy and full of sin. For this I love and thank him from my heart. Praise be to the faithful Savior, for he is so gracious and merciful as are you and the Holy Spirit in eternity. Amen.

4.

Thanksgiving for Divine Honors Bestowed on Us

Dear God, I am a poor and offensive person. Who am I that my soul is named the bride of God, and the Son of God its bridegroom?

The eternal Majesty has condescended to come into my poor flesh and blood and truly unite himself with me. This is an honor not even bestowed upon the angels in heaven. From head to foot I am full of pollution, corruption, leprosy, sin, and offense before God. How then can I be considered his beloved, and be one in body with the high, eternal, glorious Majesty? Since you want it so, oh be praised and thanked in all eternity. Amen.

5.

For Reassurance

My Lord, it does not trouble me to know who I am. Though I am wicked and sinful I know it does not make you so. You are righteous and gracious. The more wicked and sinful I am, the less I can rely on anything else, the more fervently will I implore you. This is no time to argue whether I am one of the elect or not. But I feel the need of your help, and I therefore come and seek it in all humility. Amen.

6.

Relying Solely on Christ

Dear God, the woman of Canaan was a Gentile and was not among the chosen. As she did not let this hinder her from praying, I too will pray. I need help (and must have this and that). Where else could I look and find it but with you, through your Son, my Redeemer, Jesus Christ. Amen.

7.

Obeying the Command and Trusting the Promise

Lord, you know I do not presume to come before you on my own or because of my worthiness. Were I to rely on myself I could not lift up my eyes to you. I would not know how to begin to pray. But I come because you have personally commanded and earnestly requested that we should call upon you. You have promised to hear us. You have also sent your only Son who has taught us what we are to pray and has spoken the words we are to say. So I know that this prayer pleases you. However bold I may be in your presence as a child of God, I must yield to you, for you want it so. You tell the truth. I only add to my sins and offend you more when I despise your command and doubt your promise. Amen.

8.

For Greater Faith and Diligence

Dear God, if only we were as diligent to pray, at least with a longing in the heart, as you are in coaxing, bidding, commanding, assuring, and constraining us to pray. Unfortunately, we are too lazy and ungrateful! Forgive us, dear Lord, and strengthen our faith. Since I cannot pay the penalty, and my name has no prestige, let satisfaction be made in the name of my Lord Jesus Christ. Amen.

9.

For What God Has Done and Given

O God, Creator of heaven and earth. You have sent your only Son Jesus Christ into the world. For me he was crucified, died, and was buried, and rose again on the third day. He ascended to heaven that he should sit at your right hand to rule all things. He sent his Spirit that we should await his coming to judge both the living and the dead. With the Spirit we should come to the eternal kingdom. It is our heritage which you will give us through him.

For this reason, O Lord God, you have instituted and given us Baptism and the Sacrament of the body and blood of Christ your Son. For us you have united Christ with these Sacraments. In them you reveal yourself and command us to receive you.

Cornered by Satan, we are grievously tormented by sin and constantly surrounded by death. Dear Son of God, Jesus Christ, you came to earth to destroy the work of the devil. You have brought life and immortality into the open. Give us again your work, for it is righteous and gives life. Help us to survive the attacks of the devil, by which he would throw us from life into death. O Christ, you have conquered the devil. Help me also to defeat him. Do not leave me. Amen.

10.

Dependence on Christ Alone

O heavenly Father, you have created all things and have brought the children of Israel out of Egypt, through the Red Sea, across the wilderness, and over the Jordan. All this is of no help to me. What is it to me that you have done great wonders to Noah, and enabled Peter to walk on the sea, and commanded the leper to show himself to the priest? But it is important for me to call upon you and hold fast to you. I do so by the word and assurance: You, Lord, have redeemed me through the blood of your Son, Jesus Christ. This word concerns me, for it penetrates heaven and with it I surely do touch you. You have bound yourself to it so that I might find you and cling to you. Hear me! Although neither I nor any angel can stand before your Majesty, I still have Christ whom you cannot hate. I depend on him and on the assurance that you will receive me through him. You must reject him before rejecting me. Amen.

11.

As a Dear Child of God

Lord, God, heavenly Father, I consider myself your dear child and you my beloved Father. Not because I deserve it, nor could ever merit it, but because my dear Lord, your only begotten Son Jesus Christ, would be my brother. Of his own accord he offers and makes this blessing known to me. Since I may consider myself his brother, as he regards me, you will permit me to become and remain a child of yours, forever. Amen.

12.

Assurance of Holiness through Christ

O Lord, even though I were John the Baptist, I could not give you an account of my life and deeds. I consider myself to be devout and your servant, not because of my own life and work, but because you have promised to be, and you continually are, merciful to me through Jesus Christ. If I am unholy, he is holy; if I am not a servant of God, he is God's servant; if I have cares and fears, he is free from all cares and fears. Therefore I will come in his stead and be glad that in and through him I am holy. Lord God, I am sure that I am holy in your sight, and a servant of yours. Not through myself, for I feel the guilt of my sin, but through Jesus Christ who has pardoned my sin and who has settled all for me. Praise be to you in eternity. Amen.

13.

Accepted through the Merits of Christ

Dear Lord and Father, I know beyond a doubt that you do love me, for I love your Son, my Redeemer Jesus Christ. In this trust and confidence I gladly ask you to hear me and grant what I ask. I know that you will gladly grant me all things, not because I am holy and devout, but through the merits of your Son, Jesus Christ. In his name I now come before you and ask without doubting in the least that my prayer will surely be answered, no matter who I am. Amen.

14.

Praise to God for Blessings through Jesus Christ

O Lord, I do not deserve a glimpse of heaven, and I am unable with my works to redeem myself from sin, death, the devil, and hell. Nevertheless, you have given me your Son, Jesus Christ, who is far more precious and dear than heaven, and much stronger than sin, death, the devil, and hell. For this I rejoice, praise, and thank you, O

God. Without cost and out of pure grace you have given me this
boundless blessing in your dear Son. Through him you take sin, death,
and hell from me, and do grant me all that belongs to him. Amen.

15.

For Help in the Time of Need

Dear God, in the midst of anguish and need, I am in great trouble.
My neighbors have their trials which the devil increases. This is not
the time to ask whether I am godly or worthy. Help me now in this
time of need, as you said you would. Amen.

16.

For Destruction of the Devil's Kingdom

O dear God, you are my Father. I can boldly ask all things of
you, for you cannot withhold anything from me. My heart assures me
that whatever I ask will be given. I now pray that your name and
word may be hallowed by us. At the same time I pray that you will
destroy the kingdom of the devil with all its wickedness and all that
is contrary to your Word and will. Amen.

17.

For Relief from Misery

Lord, misery and misfortune annoy me and oppress me. I long to
be rid of them. You have said, Ask and it will be given you. So I come
and ask. Amen.

18.

For an Answer to the Cry of the Helpless

Dear Lord Jesus Christ, my longing is so great that I cannot
express it in words. I know not how to ask. See my heart. What more

shall I say? My suffering is greater than all my complaining. I cannot counsel myself with reason nor comfort myself with my own courage. Comfortless, helpless, and forsaken, I am completely at loss. My God, you will not abandon my hope. You will hear my prayer and satisfy my desires. I will pray and wait for your grace. Hear me and fulfill my hope. Amen.

a. Let those who doubt they are heard of God remove their doubts and come unconfused to God in prayer. Those who doubt might as well say: Lord, I do not believe, and how can I know whether it is true when you say, "Very truly, I tell you . . . whatever you ask in my name . . . I will do." And they will treat other passages of Scripture likewise. Therefore, when you pray, kneel or stand confidently, believing your prayer will be answered, while you sincerely acknowledge yourself to be a sinner, and resolve to lead a better life.

b. We are also sufficiently taught not to tempt God in prayer. It is not for us to determine the time, measure, aim, manner, or person, and how, when, where, or through what means God must grant our requests. All this we must humbly leave to him, believing that he will rightly answer every petition according to his divine and infinite wisdom. Even if it seems otherwise, we shall not doubt that the prayer was indeed heard. When the angel Gabriel said to Daniel (Daniel 9:21-23), At the beginning of your supplications a word went out, etc., he was given far more than he had prayed for. All people shall consider themselves equally privileged to call upon God in trials of their own or others.

19.

For Assurance of Being Heard

Lord God, heavenly Father, I ask for and need assurance that my petitions may be nothing less than yes and amen. Otherwise I will not pray or have intercession made for me. Not that I am righteous or worthy, for I know very well and confess that I am unworthy. With my great and many sins I have earned your eternal wrath and hell fire.

But because you command and constrain me to pray in the name of your dear Son, our Lord Jesus Christ, I am still somewhat obedient. Not because of my own righteousness, but because of your infinite goodness, do I kneel or stand before you. I pray for what is upon my heart concerning those in need of your help. If you do not help them, O Lord, you will offend and dishonor your name. Surely you will save your reputation so that the world will not say you are an ungracious and a dreadful God. Preserve us from such misfortune.

Remember, dear heavenly Father, how you have at all times supported and helped your people. I will not stop knocking but will continue crying aloud and pleading to the end of my life. Amen.

20.

For the Father's Grace and Mercy

O God, Father in heaven, look in mercy upon your needy children, and grant us grace. Amen.

21.

That God's Name Be Hallowed

Grant us grace that your holy name may be hallowed by us throughout the world, by the pure and sincere teaching of your Word and the steady love of our life. Graciously turn aside every false doctrine and all sinful living in which your holy name is blasphemed and profaned. Amen.

22.

For the Coming of His Kingdom

In order that your kingdom may come and increase, bring all blinded sinners and those held captive by the devil to the knowledge of true faith in Jesus Christ. Make the number of souls in Christendom great. Amen.

23.

For Renewed Will

Grant that we may be strengthened by your Spirit to do and endure your will both in life and in death. May we in good and evil days give and renew our own will. Amen.

24.

For Temporal Blessings

Give us also our daily bread. Guard us against greed and anxiety for the body, that we may confidently rely on you for all blessings. Amen.

25.

For Pardon

Forgive us our debts as we forgive our debtors, so that we may have a clear and joyful conscience before you, and never again fear, nor be frightened. Amen.

26.

For Help from God's Spirit

Lead us not into temptation, but help us by your Spirit to control the flesh, to despise the world and its ways, and to dominate the devil with all his malice. Amen.

27.

For Deliverance from All Evil

Finally deliver us from all bodily and spiritual evil in time and eternity. Amen.

a. I believe without doubt that my prayer is heard and accepted in heaven, because Christ assures us: Whatever you ask for in prayer, believe that you have received it, and it will be yours.

b. Use also three devotional psalms (25, 51, 85); three comforting psalms (23, 84, 91); four psalms of thanksgiving (103, 111, 118, 138); and pray chapter 12 of Isaiah.

THE LORD'S PRAYER

*Let your kingdom come so that
sin may be expelled, and
that we may live holy and acceptable
lives in your sight.*

THE LORD'S PRAYER

28.

Seeking Our Father

Our Father in heaven, misery stands like a great wall between us. How shall we, your children on earth, so separated from you, ever come to you in our homeland? Amen.

A son honors his father, and servants their master. If then I am a father, where is the honor due? And if I am a master, where is the respect due me? Mal. 1:6. Continually, all day long, my name is despised. Is. 52:5.

29.

For God's Glory in All Things

Alas, it is so? Oh Father, we acknowledge our guilt. Be a gracious Father and do not hold us guilty, but grant us your grace so to live that your holy name may be hallowed in us. Let us in no way think, speak, do, or attempt anything unless we do so for your praise and honor. May we above all things seek your glory and not our own. Grant that as children we may love, fear, and honor you as Father. Amen.

30.

For God's Reign Within Us

O Father, unfortunately we know our bodies to be inclined to sin. The world, the flesh, and the devil wish to rule in us, and so cast out your honor and name. Therefore, we implore you, help us out of our misery. Let your kingdom come so that sin may be expelled, and that we may live holy and acceptable lives in your sight. You alone rule within us, so that with our inner and outer powers we may be obedient and be subject to you. Amen.

31.

That God's Will, Not Ours, Be Done

It grieves us that we fail to understand and receive your good help. O Father, give us grace, and let your will be done in us. Even if it hurts us, continue to correct and do whatever you desire. Your will be done, not ours. Defend us, dear Father, and let us not undertake or do anything by our own conceit, intent, and volition. Our will opposes yours. Your will alone is good, even if it does not seem good to us. Our will is evil, though it may appear good. Amen.

32.

For Bodily and Spiritual Nourishment

O Father, it is indeed true that we cannot be strong by our own power. How can we stand before your might if you do not yourself strengthen and comfort us? Therefore, dear Father, embrace us, accomplish your will in us, that we may be your kingdom to your praise and glory. But, dear Father, strengthen us in this life with your holy word. Give us our daily bread. Establish in our hearts your dear Son Jesus Christ who is the true bread of heaven. Sustained by him, we may gladly bear and suffer the breaking and the dying of our own will and the fulfilling of your will. Give grace to all your churches. Send us educated pastors and preachers who will not give us the crumbs and chaff of foolish fables, but who will teach us your holy gospel and lead us to Jesus Christ. Amen.

33.

For Forgiveness As We Forgive

O Lord, may we move you to have pity. Do not deny us our daily bread. We are sorry that we do not meet the requirements of your holy Word. We pray, be patient with us, your poor children. Forgive us our debts, and do not proceed to judge us, for in your sight no one can be justified. Remember the promise that if we gladly forgive our debtors, you will grant forgiveness. It is not that we deserve your forgiveness, but because you keep your word and have graciously promised pardon to all who forgive their neighbors. We rely on your promise. Amen.

34.

For Help to Resist Temptation

We are weak and sick, O Father, and the temptations of the flesh and the world are great and many. O Father, keep us, and let us not fall again into temptation and sin. Give us grace that we may remain steadfast and fight bravely to the end. Without your grace and help we can do nothing. Amen.

35.

For Deliverance from All Evil

Since evil blocks our way with temptation and brings us in conflict with sin, dear Father, deliver us from it. Redeemed from all sin and evil according to your will, may we belong to your kingdom to praise, honor, and hallow you forever. Amen.

36.

Assurance of Being Heard

You have taught and commanded us to pray in this manner and have promised to hear us. So we hope and are sure, O dearest Father, that for the sake of the truth you will graciously and mercifully grant us all these requests. Amen.

Someone may say: What if I could not believe that my prayers are heard? Then do like the father whose son was unable to speak, Mark 9:23, when Christ said to him, If you are able. All things can be done for the one who believes. Immediately the father of the child cried out (v. 24), "I believe; help my unbelief!"

37.

Trusting God

O God and Father, I do not doubt that the things for which I have prayed are promised, not because I prayed for them, but because you have commanded me to pray and have surely promised to grant them. God, I am certain that you keep your promise and cannot deceive us. It is not the worthiness of my prayer but the certainty of your truth that makes me firmly believe beyond doubt that it will be and remain yes and amen. Amen.

ANOTHER FORM FOR PRAYING THE LORD'S PRAYER

Our Father in heaven.

38.

For the Abiding Joy of Calling God our Father

Oh almighty God, through your infinite mercy you have not only permitted us but you have taught and commanded us to pray through your only beloved Son, our Lord Jesus Christ. By his merits and mediation we are to call you Father, though we have provoked you to anger. Be a righteous and severe judge of the sins which we so grievously and abundantly have committed against you. Mercifully pour into our hearts the comforting assurance of your fatherly love. Enable us to sense the sweetness of parental safety, so that with joy we may name you Father and call upon you in all our needs. Guard us that we may remain your children and not commit an offense by which we might prove ourselves your enemies and so make of you a dreadful judge, our most precious Father. Amen.

39.

For a United Love

It is also your will that we should not individually name you Father but together call you our Father and united pray for all. So give us a united love that we may know and consider all to be brothers and sisters. United we ask you, our beloved Father, for each and all, even as one child speaks for another to its father. Amen.

40.

For Ability to Call God "Our Father"

Let no one among us be selfish or forget others in your presence. Having discarded all hatred, envy, and discord, let us love one another as true and devout children of God, that united we may say, not "My Father," but "Our Father." Amen.

41.

For Trust in the Heavenly Father

God, you are not a father of the flesh here upon earth, but a spiritual Father in heaven, and you are not mortal, nor uncertain, nor unable to help yourself like a human father. Convince us that you are infinitely better than an earthly father. Teach us to despise temporal parentage, nationality, friends, property, flesh and blood, in comparison with you. Amen.

42.

For Grace to Be Heavenly Children

O Father, grant us also that we may be your heavenly children. Teach us to be mindful only of our souls and our heavenly heritage, so that our earthly country and inheritance may not deceive, nor limit, nor hinder us. Neither make us mere children of this world, so we may in reality call you our heavenly Father and may truly be your heavenly children. Amen.

THE FIRST PETITION

Hallowed be your name.

43.

Against Profaning God's Name

Almightly God, dear heavenly Father, in this miserable valley of tears your name is so often profaned, blasphemed, and reviled. Because of many things without your honor, and taken in vain for sinful reasons, this harmful life is indeed a disgrace and a dishonor to your holy name. Therefore give us your grace that we may guard ourselves against all that does not contribute to the honor and praise of your holy name. Help us to abolish all profanity and deceitful blessings. Grant that all conjuring in your name by ungodly people and the devil may cease. Assist us in uprooting every false belief and superstition. Wipe out all heresy and wrong teaching disguised in your name. Grant that all false imitation of truth, devotion, and holiness may deceive no one. Amen.

44.

For Help to Glorify God Alone

Help that no one may perjure, lie, or deceive by your name. Preserve us from every false comfort fabricated under the disguise of your name. Guard us against all spiritual pride and vanity of earthly glory or distinction. Help us to call upon you in all our needs and weaknesses. Assure us that in the distress of our conscience, and in the hour of death, we may not forget your name. Help us that with all our possessions, words, and works we may praise and honor only you, and not through them seek to win a name for ourselves. We glorify you alone to whom all things belong. Guard us against the shameful evil of ingratitude. Amen.

45.

For Help to Avoid Offense

Help us so that by our lives and good works others may be prompted not to exalt us but to praise you in us and to honor your name. Grant that no one may be offended by our evil works or short-comings, and so dishonor you and praise you less. Keep us from desiring anything temporal or eternal that does not praise and honor your name. If we should ask you for any such things, we pray that you would not hear our foolishness. Help us so to live that we may be found true children of God, and that your fatherly name may not be used falsely or in vain because of us. Amen.

THE SECOND PETITION

Your kingdom come.

46.

For Faith, Hope, and Love

This miserable life is a kingdom of all sin and evil, in which the devil is lord, the source and the chief servant of all wickedness. But your kingdom is a kingdom of every grace and virtue in which the only Lord is Jesus Christ, your dear Son, the one head and source of every blessing. Therefore, grant us your grace and help, dear Father. Give us above all else a true and lasting faith in Christ and a fearless hope in your mercy. In place of every weakness of our sinful conscience, give us a fervent and blessed love toward you and all people. Guard us against unbelief, despair, and all envy. Amen.

47.

For Virtue, Peace, Unity, Etc.

Purify us of unchastity, and give us a high regard for all things that are clean. Deliver us from discord, strife, and warfare. Grant to us the virtue, peace, unity, and quiet rest of your kingdom. Strengthen us that neither anger nor any other bitterness can defeat your kingdom within us. Help that through your grace we may be controlled by a sweet disposition, a trusting confidence, and every manner of kindness, goodness, and meekness. Preserve us from excessive grief and sorrow. Let the joy and pleasure of your grace and mercy come to us. Amen.

48.

To Serve God with Thoughts, Affections, and Will

Ultimately turn from us all sins. By your grace fill us with all virtue and good works. Help us to become your kingdom. Grant that we may with all our thoughts, affections, and will, and with all bodily and spiritual strength, obediently serve you according to your will and commandments. Permit these powers to be ruled only by you, and not to obey themselves, the flesh, the world, and the devil. Amen.

49.

For Extension of God's Kingdom

Help your kingdom to begin and grow in us and daily to further and extend itself. Let not deceptive wickedness and inactivity subdue us in your service. Keep us from backsliding. Give us a firm resolve and ability not merely to begin being devout but to continue boldly and to win, as the psalmist says: "Give light to my eyes, or I will sleep the sleep of death, and my enemy will say, I have prevailed" (Psalm 13:3-4). Amen.

50.

For the Coming Kingdom

Help us to remain so steadfast that your coming kingdom will include and complete your kingdom begun here. Lead us out of this sinful and dangerous life. Help us to be willing to let go of this life and to long for the life that is to come. Enable us not to dread death but to welcome it. Release us from the love and attachments of this life, so that your kingdom may be totally completed in us. Amen.

THE THIRD PETITION

Your will be done, on earth as in heaven.

51.

For the Surrender of Self-will to God's Will

Our will compared with your will is not good but continually evil. Your will is always by far the best, the most highly cherished, and to be desired by us. Therefore, be merciful to us, dear Father, and let not anything be done according to our will. When our will is hindered or broken, teach us true patience. Grant that we may not become angry or malicious when anyone speaks or is silent, does anything or leaves anything undone against our will. Oh may we not curse, complain, cry out, judge, condemn, or protest. Help us humbly to yield or surrender our will to those who oppose and hinder us and who accomplish your divine and most blessed will in spite of us. May we praise and bless them and do good to them. Amen.

52.

For God's Will to Control Our Will

Give us grace to willingly acknowledge and bear all sickness, poverty, shame, suffering, and misfortune as coming from your divine will to crucify ours. Grant that we may gladly suffer injury, and guard us against seeking revenge. Let us not repay evil with evil, nor oppose force with force. But let us have pleasure in your will which permits these to come upon us, and let us give praise and thanks to you.

When something opposes our will, let us not attribute it to the devil or wicked people, but to your will which regulates all things that they might hinder our will and that your kingdom may be blessed.

According to your will, help us not to be disobedient through impatience and despair but to leave this life cheerfully and obediently.

Help that our eyes, tongue, heart, hands, feet, and bodily organs may not be left to their own inclinations but be held, bound, and controlled by your will. Guard us against our own stubborn, cruel, obstinate, selfish will. Amen.

53.

For a Charitable Disposition

Give us true obedience and perfect resignation in all things temporal and eternal. Preserve us from the cruel vice of slandering, defaming, judging, and condemning others. Oh that the great misery and harm caused by such tongues were far from us! When we see or hear anything of others that seems blamable and disagreeable to us, teach us to cover it up and to keep silent about it. Help us to complain to you alone and leave all to your will, and so gladly to forgive all our debtors and sympathize with them. Amen.

54.

For Compassion to Those Who Offend Us

Teach us to realize that people cannot harm us without in so doing hurting themselves a thousand times more in your sight. So may we show compassion more than anger toward those who offend us, and pity rather than punish them. Help us not to rejoice when misfortune comes to those who have not done our will, or who in some other way have displeased us with their lives. May we not grieve when they prosper. Amen.

THE FOURTH PETITION

Give us today our daily bread.

55.

For Spiritual Nurture

This bread is our Lord Jesus Christ who feeds and comforts the soul. Therefore, oh heavenly Father, grant us grace that the life, words, works, and sufferings of Christ may be preached, made known, and preserved for us and all the world. Help us to keep his words and works in all walks of life as a powerful example and an inducement to every virtue. Enable us in our sufferings and tribulations to be strengthened and comforted by his sufferings and cross. Help us to conquer our death by a firm faith in his victory over death and boldly follow our beloved Leader into the life beyond. Amen.

56.

For Faithful Pastors and All in Authority

Give grace to all preachers to proclaim Christ and your Word in all the world profitably and gladly. Grant that all who hear your Word preached may learn to know Christ and actually improve their lives through him. Exclude from your holy church all strange doctrines and preaching in which Christ is not made known. Be merciful to all bishops and ministers and all in authority, that they may be enlightened by your grace and rightly teach and lead us by good word and good example. Protect all who are weak in the faith that they may not be misled by the wickedness of any in authority. Amen.

57.

For Grace to Receive the Sacraments Worthily

Preserve us from false and dangerous doctrines, so that as we eat our daily bread we may remain united in the teachings of Jesus Christ.

Teach us by grace rightly to regard the sufferings of Christ, gladly to embrace them, and cheerfully to regulate our lives according to them. Let not the holy body of Christ be withheld from us as we face death. Grant that we and all Christians may worthily receive the holy sacraments in due season. Amen.

58.

For Universal Peace

Grant us blessed unity and peace among all nations. Preserve us from all strife, hatred, and warfare, that we may eat our daily bread and receive bodily nourishment undisturbed and to your praise. Give understanding and a loyal will to all kings, princes, lords, and councils and to all in positions of government, that they may rule their people in a happy and peaceful way. Guard all citizens against rebellion and disobedience. Amen.

59.

For Preservation of Home and Property

Teach us by your Spirit to manage our homes well and to rule our households in a Christian manner, to your service, praise, and glory. Preserve our children and all in our household from sin and shame, as well as from danger and harm to body and soul. Protect the fruits of the fields and all cattle from lightning, poison, wild beasts, and every possible injury. Amen.

60.

For Relief of the Distressed

Graciously comfort and tend all who are imprisoned, hungry, thirsty, naked, and miserable; also all widows, orphans, sick, and sorrowing. In brief, give us our daily bread, so that Christ may abide in us and we in him, forever, and that with him we may worthily bear the name Christian. Amen.

THE FIFTH PETITION

Forgive us our sins, as we forgive those who sin against us.

61.

For Removal of Guilt and the Fear of Judgment

O Father, relieve our consciences, now and in the hour of death, from the terror of our guilt and the fear of your judgment. Let your peace come into our hearts that we may await your judgment with joy. Be not severe in your judgment of us, or no one will be found righteous. Teach us, dear Father, not to trust or find comfort in our own merits or good works. But teach us to venture and resign ourselves faithfully and firmly to your infinite mercy. In the same manner let us not lose courage because of our sinful and guilty lives. Let us regard your mercy as higher and broader and stronger than all our being. Amen.

62.

For Help in Struggle with Death

Help all people, especially those struggling with death and who are tempted to despair. Comfort and receive them by your pardoning grace. Forgive each one of us our trespasses. Amen.

63.

For False Accusers

As you have promised, give us your goodness in place of our wickedness. Silence all cruel slanderers and accusers, those who magnify our faults, and the devil. Do so now and whenever our conscience is worried. Keep us from all backbiting and from exaggerating the sins of others. Judge us not by the evidence of the devil and by our own depressed consciences. Hear not the cry of our enemies who accuse us day and night before you, just as we would not listen to the slandering and accusing of others. Take from our souls the heavy burden of all our sins, so that with a clear, joyful, and sincere conscience we may endure and do all things, and live and die fully confident of your mercy. Amen.

THE SIXTH PETITION

Save us from the time of trial.

64.

For Strength to Overcome the Lusts of the Flesh

We have the three tempters: the flesh, the world, and the devil. Therefore, dear Father, we ask you to give us the grace to expel the lusts of the flesh. Help us to avoid excessive eating, drinking, and sleeping, and to resist laziness.

Grant that by fasting, careful eating, and proper clothing and care for the body we may watch and toil to become useful and fitted for good works. Help us to kill and to crucify with Christ's help all evil inclinations and lusts of the flesh, with all its cravings and temptations, so that no one will concede to its temptations or follow them.

Help that when we see a beautiful person or creature we may not be led to temptation but to admiration and to praising you through your creation. Grant that when we hear something pleasant and perceive something lovely we may not seek lust in it but rather praise and glory. Amen.

65.

For Protection from Greed

Preserve us from a corrupt desire and greed for the wealth of the world. Guard us from seeking the power and glory of this world and succumbing in its views. Protect us from the treachery of the world, so that its deception and wealth may not entice us to follow it. Amen.

66.

For Help to Renounce the World

Strengthen us so that the evil and misfortune of the world may not lead us into impatience, anger, revenge, or other wrongs. As we have vowed to you in Baptism, help us to renounce the lies, deceptions, false promises, and perjuries of the world, and all its good and evil. Enable us to remain true to this vow and daily to improve our lives. Amen.

67.

For Protection Against Temptation

Preserve us from the forces of the devil. Let us not sanction pride, our own pleasures, and other detractions, for the sake of riches, fame, power, skill, popularity, or any other gift of yours. Guard us against yielding to hatred and envy for any cause. Preserve us now and until our last moment from following the disputes of faith and the despair that follows. Amen.

68.

For Strength to Overcome the Enemies of Faith

Heavenly Father, may we commend to you all who strive and work against great and many temptations. Strengthen those who still stand. Restore those who have fallen and given up. Grant all of us your grace in a miserable and uncertain life, and though surrounded constantly by so many enemies, may we persistently fight with a valiant and firm faith and finally obtain the eternal crown. Amen.

THE SEVENTH PETITION

And deliver us from evil.

69.

For Deliverance from God's Wrath

O Father, deliver us from your eternal wrath and from the torture of hell. Save us from your severe judgment in death and at the last day. Guard us against sudden and eternal death. Preserve us from the misery of fire and water, hail and lightning, need and hunger. Amen.

70.

For Protection from Disease and Tragedies

Protect us from war, bloodshed, plagues, pestilence, and other grievous diseases. Guard us against all evil and distress of the body. Let your kingdom and the glory of your name be fulfilled in all these things. Amen.

71.

For Assurance of Being Heard

Amen. Oh God help that we may without faltering do all these petitions. Let us never doubt that you have heard us and will hear us again in this prayer, and that it shall be yes and not no nor maybe. Therefore we gladly say amen, which means true and certain. Amen.

A Simple Way to Pray

*We must be careful not to break
the habit of true prayer and
imagine other works to be necessary
which, after all, are nothing of
the kind.*

A SIMPLE WAY TO PRAY

How One Should Pray
For Peter, the Master Barber

Luther wrote these instructions when Peter, his barber, inquired of him how an ordinary person could pray without being disturbed by worldly thoughts and occupations. He included a brief explanation of the Lord's Prayer, the Ten Commandments, and the Apostles' Creed.

Dear Master Peter: I will tell you as best I can what I do personally when I pray. May our dear Lord grant to you and to everybody to do it better than I! Amen.

First, when I feel that I have become cool and joyless in prayer because of other tasks or thoughts (for the flesh and the devil always impede and obstruct prayer), I take my little psalter, hurry to my room, or, if it be the day and hour for it, to the church where a congregation is assembled and, as time permits, I say quietly to myself and word-for-word the Ten Commandments, the Creed, and, if I have time, some words of Christ or of Paul, or some psalms, just as a child might do.

It is a good thing to let prayer be the first business of the morning and the last at night. Guard yourself carefully against those false, deluding ideas which tell you, "Wait a little while. I will pray in an hour; first I must attend to this or that." Such thoughts get you away from prayer into other affairs which so hold your attention and involve you that nothing comes of prayer for that day.

It may well be that you may have some tasks which are as good or better than prayer, especially in an emergency. There is a saying ascribed to St. Jerome that everything a believer does is prayer and a proverb, "Those who work faithfully pray twice." This can be said because believers fear and honor God in their work and remember the commandment not to wrong anyone, or to try to steal, defraud, or cheat. Such thoughts and such faith undoubtedly transform their work into prayer and a sacrifice of praise.

On the other hand it is also true that the work of unbelievers is outright cursing and so those who work faithlessly curse twice. While they do their work their thoughts are occupied with a neglect of God and violation of his law, how to take advantage of their neighbors, how to steal from them and defraud them. What else can such thoughts be but out-and-out curses against God and humanity, which make such persons' work and effort a double curse by which they curse themselves. In the end they are beggars and bunglers. It is of such continual, prayer that Christ says in Luke 11, "Pray without ceasing" (1 Thess. 5:17. See Luke 11:9-13), because one must unceasingly guard against sin and wrong-doing, something one cannot do unless one fears God and keeps his commandment in mind, as Psalm 1 [:1, 2] says, "Blessed are those . . . who meditate on his law day and night."

Yet we must be careful not to break the habit of true prayer and imagine other works to be necessary which, after all, are nothing of the kind. Thus at the end we become lax and lazy, cool and listless toward prayer. The devil who besets us is not lazy or careless, and our flesh is too ready and eager to sin and is disinclined to the spirit of prayer.

When your heart has been warmed by such recitation to yourself [of the Ten Commandments, the words of Christ, etc.] and is intent upon the matter, kneel or stand with your hands folded and your eyes toward heaven and speak or think as briefly as you can:

72.

Prayer According to God's Command and Promise

O heavenly Father, dear God, I am a poor unworthy sinner. I do not deserve to raise my eyes or hands toward you or to pray. But because you have commanded us all to pray and have promised to hear us and through your dear Son Jesus Christ have taught us both how and what to pray, I come to you in obedience to your word, trusting in your gracious promise. I pray in the name of my Lord

Jesus Christ together with all your saints and Christians on earth as he has taught us:

Our Father in heaven.
Hallowed be your name.
Your kingdom come.
Your will be done on earth as in heaven.
Give us today our daily bread.
And forgive us our sins, as we forgive those who sin against us.
Save us from the time of trial.
And deliver us from evil. Amen.

THE FIRST PETITION

Hallowed be your name.

73.

For the Destruction of False Teachings

"Yes, Lord God, dear Father, hallowed be your name, both in us and throughout the whole world. Destroy and root out the abominations, idolatry, and heresy of all false teachers and fanatics who wrongly use your name and in scandalous ways take it in vain (Ex. 20:7) and horribly blaspheme it. They insistently boast that they teach your word and the laws of the church, though they really use the devil's deceit and trickery in your name to wretchedly seduce many poor souls throughout the world, even killing and shedding much innocent blood, and in such persecution they believe that they render you a divine service.

74.

For Conversion and Restraint

Dear Lord God, convert and restrain them. Convert those who are still to be converted that they with us and we with them may hallow and praise your name, both with true and pure doctrine and

with a good and holy life. Restrain those who are unwilling to be
converted so that they be forced to cease from misusing, defiling, and
dishonoring your holy name and from misleading the poor people.
Amen.

THE SECOND PETITION

Your kingdom come.

75.

For Protection and Extension of God's Kingdom

O dear Lord, God and Father, you see how worldly wisdom and
reason not only profane your name and ascribe the honor due to you
to lies and to the devil, but how they also take the power, might,
wealth and glory which you have given them on earth for ruling the
world and thus serving you, and use it in their own ambition to oppose
your kingdom. They are many and mighty; they plague and hinder
the tiny flock of your kingdom who are weak, despised, and few. They
will not tolerate your flock on earth and think that by plaguing them
they render a great and godly service to you.

Dear Lord, God and Father, convert them and defend us. Convert
those who are still to become children and members of your kingdom
so that they with us and we with them may serve you in your kingdom
in true faith and unfeigned love and that from your kingdom which
has begun, we may enter into your eternal kingdom. Defend us against
those who will not turn away their might and power from the de-
struction of your kingdom so that when they are cast down from their
thrones and humbled, they will have to cease from their efforts. Amen.

THE THIRD PETITION

Your will be done on earth as in heaven.

76.

For Help to Do God's Will

O dear Lord, God and Father, you know that the world, if it cannot destroy your name or root out your kingdom, is busy day and night with wicked tricks and schemes, strange conspiracies and intrigue, huddling together in secret counsel, giving mutual encouragement and support, raging and threatening and going about with every evil intention to destroy your name, word, kingdom, and children. Therefore, dear Lord, God and Father, convert them and defend us. Convert those who have yet to acknowledge your good will that they with us and we with them may obey your will and for your sake gladly, patiently, and joyously bear every evil, cross, and adversity, and thereby acknowledge, test, and experience your benign, gracious and perfect will. But defend us against those who in their rage, fury, hate, threats, and evil desires do not cease to do us harm. Make their wicked schemes, tricks, and devices to come to nothing so that these may be turned against them, as we sing in Psalm 7 [:16].[1]

THE FOURTH PETITION

Give us today our daily bread.

77.

For Peace and Good Government

Dear Lord, God and Father, grant us your blessing also in this temporal and physical life. Graciously grant us blessed peace. Protect

---

[1]"His mischief returns upon his own head, and on his own pate his violence descends."

us against war and disorder. Grant to our dear emperor fortune and success against his enemies. Grant him wisdom and understanding to rule over his earthly kingdom in peace and prosperity. Grant to all rulers good counsel and the will to preserve their domains and their subjects in tranquillity and justice. Amen.

78.

For Protection of Home and Family

Oh, God, grant that all people—in city and country—be diligent and display charity and loyalty toward each other. Give us favorable weather and good harvest. I commend to you my house and property, wife and children. Grant that I may manage and guide them well, supporting and educating them as a Christian should. Defend us against the Destroyer and all his wicked angels who would do us harm and mischief in this life. Amen.

THE FIFTH PETITION

Forgive us our sins as we forgive those who sin against us.

79.

For God's Mercy

O dear Lord, God and Father, enter not into judgment against us because no person living is justified before you. Do not count it against us as a sin that we are so unthankful for your ineffable goodness, spiritual and physical, or that we stray into sin many times every day, more often than we can know or recognize, Psalm 19 [:12]. Do not look upon how good or how wicked we have been but only upon the infinite compassion which you have bestowed upon us in Christ, your dear Son. Amen.

80.

For Our Enemies

Also grant forgiveness to those who have harmed or wronged us, as we forgive them from our hearts. They inflict the greatest injury upon themselves by arousing your anger in their actions toward us. We are not helped by their ruin; we would much rather that they be saved with us. Amen.

THE SIXTH PETITION

Save us from the time of trial.

81.

For Triumph Over the Devil

"Oh dear Lord, Father and God, keep us fit and alert, eager and diligent in your word and service, so that we do not become complacent, lazy, and slothful as though we had already achieved everything. In that way the fearful devil cannot fall upon us, surprise us, and deprive us of your precious word or stir up strife and factions among us and lead us into other sin and disgrace, both spiritually and physically. Rather grant us wisdom and strength through your spirit that we may valiantly resist him and gain the victory. Amen.

THE SEVENTH PETITION

And deliver us from evil.

82.

For Help to Pass Safely through Dangers

"O dear Lord, God and Father, this wretched life is so full of misery and calamity, of danger and uncertainty, so full of malice and faithlessness (as St. Paul says in Ephesians 5:16, "The days are evil" that we might rightfully grow weary of life and long for death. But you, dear Father, know our frailty; therefore help us to pass in safety through so much wickedness and villainy; and, when our last hour comes, in your mercy grant us a blessed departure from this vale of sorrows so that in the face of death we do not become fearful or despondent but in firm faith commit our souls into your hands. Amen."

Amen

Finally, mark this, that you must always speak the Amen firmly. Never doubt that God in his mercy will surely hear you and say "yes" to your prayers. Never think that you are kneeling or standing alone, rather think that the whole of Christendom, all devout Christians, are standing there beside you and you are standing among them in a common, united petition which God cannot disdain. Do not leave your prayer without having said or thought, "Very well, God has heard my prayer; this I know as a certainty and a truth." That is what Amen means.

You should also know that I do not want you to recite all these words in your prayer. That would make it nothing but idle chatter and prattle. Rather do I want your heart to be stirred and guided concerning the thoughts which ought to be comprehended in the Lord's Prayer. These thoughts may be expressed, if your heart is rightly warmed and inclined toward prayer, in many different ways and with more words or fewer.

I do not bind myself to such words or syllables, but say my prayers in one fashion today, in another tomorrow, depending upon my mood and feeling. I stay however, as nearly as I can, with the same general thoughts and ideas. It may happen occasionally that I may get lost among so many ideas in one petition that I forego the other six.

If such an abundance of good thoughts comes to us we ought to disregard the other petitions, make room for such thoughts, listen in silence, and under no circumstances obstruct them. The Holy Spirit himself preaches here, and one word of his sermon is far better than a thousand of our prayers. Many times I have learned more from one prayer than I might have learned from much reading and speculation.

It is of great importance that the heart be made ready and eager for prayer. As Sirach says, "Prepare your heart for prayer, and do not tempt God" *[*Sirach 18:23*]*. What else is it but tempting God when your mouth babbles and the mind wanders to other thoughts? Like the cleric who prayed, *"Deus in adjutorium meum intende.*[2] Farmhand, did you unhitch the horses? *Domine ad adjuvandum me festina.*[3] Maid, go out and milk the cow. *Gloria patri et filio et spiritui sancto.*[4] Hurry up, boy, I wish the ague would take you!" I have heard many such prayers in the past. This is blasphemy and it would be better if they played at it if they cannot or do not care to do better. In my day I have prayed many such canonical hours myself, regrettably, and in such a manner that the psalm or the allotted time came to an end before I even realized whether I was at the beginning or the middle.

Though not all of them blurt out the words as did the above-mentioned cleric and mix business and prayer, they do it by the thoughts in their hearts. They jump from one thing to another in their thoughts and when it is all over they do not know what they have done or what they talked about. They start with *Laudate*[5] and right away they are in a fool's paradise.

It seems to me that if we could see what arises as prayer from a cold and unattentive heart we would conclude that we had never seen a more ridiculous kind of buffoonery. But, praise God, it is now clear to me that those who forget what they have said have not prayed well. In a good prayer one fully remembers every word and thought from the beginning to the end of the prayer.

So, a good and attentive barber keeps his thoughts, attention, and eyes on the razor and hair and does not forget how far he has gotten with his shaving or cutting. If he wants to engage in too much conversation or let his mind wander or look somewhere else, he is likely

[2]"Make haste, O God to deliver me." Ps. 70:1.
[3]"Make haste to help me, O Lord."
[4]"Glory be to the Father and to the Son and to the Holy Ghost."
[5]"Praise."

A Simple Way to Pray

to cut his customer's mouth, nose, or even his throat. Thus if anything is to be done well, it requires the full attention of all one's senses and members, as the proverb says, *"Pluribus intentus, minor est ad singula sensus"*—"The one who thinks of many things, thinks of nothing and does nothing right." How much more does prayer call for concentration and singleness of heart if it is to be a good prayer!

This in short is the way I use the Lord's Prayer when I pray it. To this day I suckle at the Lord's Prayer like a child, and as an old man eat and drink from it and never get my fill. It is the very best prayer, even better than the psalter, which is so very dear to me. It is surely evident that a real master composed and taught it. What a great pity that the prayer of such a master is prattled and chattered so irreverently all over the world! How many pray the Lord's Prayer several thousand times in the course of a year, and if they were to keep on doing so for a thousand years they would not have tasted nor prayed one iota, one dot,[6] of it! In a word, the Lord's Prayer is the greatest martyr on earth (as are the name and word of God). Everybody tortures and abuses it; few take comfort and joy in its proper use.

THE TEN COMMANDMENTS

If I have had time and opportunity to go through the Lord's Prayer, I do the same with the Ten Commandments. I take one part after another and free myself as much as possible from distractions in order to pray. I divide each commandment into four parts, thereby fashioning a garland of four strands. That is, I think of each commandment as, first, instruction, which is really what it is intended to be, and consider what the Lord God demands of me so earnestly. Second, I turn it into a thanksgiving; third, a confession; and fourth, a prayer. I do so in thoughts or words such as these:

The First Commandment

"I am the Lord your God. You shall have no other gods."

Here I earnestly consider that God expects and teaches me to trust him sincerely in all things and that it is his most earnest purpose

[6]"Jot and tittle." Matt. 5:18 (KJV).

to be my God. I must think of him in this way at the risk of losing eternal salvation. My heart must not build upon anything else or trust in any other thing, be it wealth, prestige, wisdom, might, piety, or anything else.

Second, I give thanks for his infinite compassion by which he has come to me in such a fatherly way and, unasked, unbidden, and unmerited, has offered to be my God, to care for me, and to be my comfort, guardian, help, and strength in every time of need. We poor mortals have sought so many gods and would have to seek them still if he did not enable us to hear him openly tell us in our own language that he intends to be our God. How could we ever—in all eternity—thank him enough!

Third, I confess and acknowledge my great sin and ingratitude for having so shamefully despised such sublime teachings and such a precious gift throughout my whole life, and for having fearfully provoked his wrath by countless acts of idolatry. I repent of these and ask for his grace.

83.

For Grace to Learn and Live

"O my God and Lord, help me by the grace to learn and understand thy commandments more fully every day and to live by them in sincere confidence. Preserve my heart so that I shall never again become forgetful and ungrateful, that I may never seek after other gods or other consolation on earth or in any creature, but cling truly and solely to thee, my only God. Amen, dear Lord God and Father. Amen."

The Second Commandment

Afterward, if time and inclination permit, the Second Commandment likewise in four strands, like this: "You shall not take the name of the Lord your God in vain."

First, I learn that I must keep God's name in honor, holiness, and beauty; not to swear, curse, not to be boastful or seek honor and repute for myself, but humbly to invoke his name, to pray, praise, and extol it, and to let it be my only honor and glory that he is my God and that I am his lowly creature and unworthy servant.

Second, I give thanks to him for these precious gifts, that he has revealed his name to me and bestowed it upon me, that I can glory in his name and be called God's servant and creature, that his name is my refuge like a mighty fortress to which the righteous person can flee and find protection, as Solomon says [Prov. 18:10].

Third, I confess and acknowledge that I have grievously and shamefully sinned against this commandment all my life. I have not only failed to invoke, extol, and honor his holy name, but have also been ungrateful for such gifts and have, by swearing, lying, and betraying, misused them in the pursuit of shame and sin. This I bitterly regret and ask grace and forgiveness.

Fourth, I ask for help and strength henceforth to learn [to obey] this commandment and to be preserved from such evil ingratitude, abuse, and sin against his name.

The Third Commandment

"Remember the sabbath day, to keep it holy."

I learned from this, first of all, that the sabbath day has not been instituted for the sake of being idle or indulging in worldly pleasures, but in order that we may keep it holy. However, it is not sanctified by our works and actions—our works are not holy—but by the word of God, which alone is wholly pure and sacred and which sanctifies everything that comes in contact with it, be it time, place, person, labor, rest, etc. According to St. Paul, who says that every creature is consecrated by word and prayer, 1 Timothy 4:5, our works are consecrated through the word. I realized therefore that on the sabbath I must, above all, hear and contemplate God's word. Thereafter I should give thanks in my own words, praise God for all his benefits, and pray for myself and for the whole world.

Second, I thank God in this commandment for his great and beautiful goodness and grace which he has given us in the preaching of his word. And he has instructed us to make use of it, especially on the sabbath day, for the meditation of the human heart can never exhaust such a treasure. His word is the only light in the darkness of this life, a word of life, consolation, and supreme blessedness. Where this precious and saving word is absent, nothing remains but a fearsome and terrifying darkness, error and faction, death and every calamity, and the tyranny of the devil himself, as we can see with our own eyes every day.

Third, I confess and acknowledge great sin and wicked ingratitude on my part because all my life I have made disgraceful use of the sabbath and have thereby despised his precious and dear word in a wretched way. I have been too lazy, listless, and uninterested to listen to it, let alone to have desired it sincerely or to have been grateful for it. I have let my dear God proclaim his word to me in vain, have dismissed the noble treasure, and have trampled it underfoot. He has tolerated this in his great and divine mercy and has not ceased in his fatherly, divine love and faithfulness to keep on preaching to me and calling me to the salvation of my soul. For this I repent and ask for grace and forgiveness.

Fourth, I pray for myself and for the whole world that the gracious Father may preserve us in his holy word and not withdraw it from us because of our sin, ingratitude, and laziness. May he preserve us from divisive spirits and false teachers, and may he send faithful and honest laborers into his harvest [Matt. 9:38], that is, devout pastors and preachers. May he grant us grace humbly to hear, accept, and honor their words as his own words and to offer our sincere thanks and praise.

The Fourth Commandment

"Honor your father and your mother."

First, I learn to acknowledge God, my Creator; how wondrously he has created me, body and soul; and how he has given me life through my parents and has instilled in them the desire to care for me, the fruit of their bodies, with all their power. He has brought me into this world, has sustained and cared for me, nurtured and educated me with great diligence, carefulness, and concern, through danger, trouble, and hard work. To this moment he protects me, his creature, and helps me in countless dangers and troubles. It is as though he were creating me anew every moment. But the devil does not willingly concede us one single moment of life.

Second, I thank the rich and gracious Creator on behalf of myself and all the world that he has established and assured in the commandment the increase and preservation of the human race, that is, of households and of states. Without these two institutions or governments the world could not exist a single year, because without government there can be no peace, and where there is no peace there can be no family; without family, children cannot be begotten or raised, and fatherhood and motherhood would cease to be.

It is the purpose of this commandment to guard and preserve both family and state, to admonish children and subjects to be obedient, and to enforce it, too, and to let no violation go unpunished—otherwise children would have disrupted the family long ago by their disobedience, and subjects would have disorganized the state and laid it to waste for they outnumber parents and rulers. There are no words to fully describe the benefit of this commandment.

Third, I confess and lament my wicked disobedience and sin; in defiance of God's commandment I have not honored or obeyed my parents; I have often provoked and offended them, have been impatient with their parental discipline, have been resentful and scornful of their loving admonition and have rather gone along with loose company and evil companions. God himself condemns such disobedient children and withholds from them a long life; many of them succumb and perish in disgrace before they reach adulthood. Whoever does not obey father and mother must obey the executioner or otherwise come, through God's wrath, to an evil end. Of all this I repent and ask for grace and forgiveness.

Fourth, I pray for myself and for all the world that God would bestow his grace and pour his blessing richly upon the family and the state. Grant that from this time on we may be devout, honor our parents, obey our superiors, and resist the devil when he entices us to be disobedient and rebellious, and so may we help improve home and nation by our actions and thus preserve the peace, all to the praise and glory of God for our own benefit and for the prosperity of all. Grant that we may acknowledge these his gifts and be thankful for them.

At this point we should add a prayer for our parents and superiors, that God may grant them understanding and wisdom to govern and rule us in peace and happiness. May he preserve them from tyranny, from riot and fury, and turn them to honor God's word and not oppress it, nor persecute anyone or do injustice. Such excellent gifts must be sought by prayer, as St. Paul teaches; otherwise the devil will reign in the palace and everything fall into chaos and confusion.

If you are a father or mother, you should at this point remember your children and the workers in your household. Pray earnestly to the dear Father, who has set you in an office of honor in his name and intends that you be honored by the name "father." Ask that he grant you grace and blessing to look after and support your wife, children, and servants in a godly and Christian manner. May he give you wisdom and strength to guide and train them well in heart and will to follow your instruction with obedience. Both are God's gifts, your children and the way they flourish, that they turn out well and that they remain so. Otherwise the home is nothing but a pigsty and school for rascals, as one can see among the uncouth and godless.

The Fifth Commandment

"You shall not kill." Here I learn, first of all, that God desires me to love my neighbors, so that I do them no bodily harm, either by word or action, neither injure nor take revenge upon them in anger, vexation, envy, hatred, or for any evil reason, but realize that I am obliged to assist and counsel them in every bodily need. In this commandment God commands me to protect my neighbor's body and in turn commands my neighbor to protect my own.

Second, I give thanks for such ineffable love, providence, and faithfulness toward me by which he has placed this mighty shield and wall to protect my physical safety. All are obliged to care for me and protect me, and I, in turn, must behave likewise toward others. He upholds this command and, where it is not observed, he has established the sword as punishment for those who do not live up to it. Were it not for this excellent commandment and ordinance, the devil would instigate such a massacre among us that no one could live in safety for a single hour—as happens when God becomes angry and inflicts punishment upon a disobedient and ungrateful world.

Third, I confess and lament my own wickedness and that of the world, not only that we are so terribly ungrateful for such fatherly love and solicitude toward us—but what is especially scandalous, that we do not acknowledge this commandment and teaching, are unwilling to learn it, and neglect it as though it did not concern us or we had no part in it. We amble along complacently, feel no remorse that in defiance of this commandment we neglect our neighbors, and, yes, we desert them, persecute, injure, or even kill them in our thoughts. We indulge in anger, rage, and villainy as though we were doing a fine and noble thing. Really, it is high time that we started to deplore and bewail how much we have acted like rogues and like unseeing, unruly, and unfeeling persons who kick, scratch, tear, and devour one another like furious beasts and pay no heed to this serious and divine command.

Fourth, I pray the dear Father to lead us to an understanding of this his sacred commandment and to help us keep it and live in accordance with it. May he preserve us from the murderer who is the master of every form of murder and violence. May he grant us his grace that we and all others may treat each other in kindly, gentle, charitable ways, forgiving one another from the heart, bearing each other's faults and shortcomings, and thus living together in true peace and concord, as the commandment teaches and requires us to do.

The Sixth Commandment

"You shall not commit adultery." Here I learn once more what God intends and expects me to do, namely, to live chastely, decently, and temperately, both in thoughts and in words and actions, and not to disgrace any one's spouse, son or daughter, or member of the household. More than this, I ought to assist, save, protect, and guard marriage and decency to the best of my ability; I should silence the idle thoughts of those who want to destroy and slander their reputation.

All this I am obliged to do and God expects me not only to leave the families of my neighbors unmolested, but I owe it to my neighbors to preserve and protect their good character and honor, just as I would want my neighbors to do for me and mine in keeping with this commandment.

Second, I thank my faithful and dear Father for his grace and benevolence by which he accepts my husband, wife, son, daughter, and servant into his care and protect and forbids so sternly and firmly anything that would bring them into disrepute. He protects and upholds this commandment and does not leave violations unpunished, even though he himself has to act if someone disregards and violates the commandment and precept.

God desires chastity and will not tolerate adultery. That can be seen every day when the impenitent and profligate are overtaken by the wrath of God and perish miserably. Otherwise it would be impossible to guard one's spouse, children, and servants against the devil's filthiness for a single hour or preserve them in honor and decency. What would happen would be unbridled immorality and beastliness, as happens when God in his wrath withdraws his hand and permits everything to go to wrack and ruin.

Third, I confess and acknowledge my sin, my own and that of all the world, how I have sinned against this commandment my whole life in thought, word, and action. Not only have I been ungrateful for these excellent teachings and gifts, but I have complained and rebelled against the divine requirement of such decency and chastity, that God has not permitted all sorts of fornication and rascality to go unchecked and unpunished. He will not allow marriage to be despised, ridiculed, or condemned, etc. Sins against this commandment are, above all others, the grossest and most conspicuous and cannot be covered up or whitewashed. For this I am sorry.

Fourth, I pray for myself and all the world that God may grant us grace to keep this commandment gladly and cheerfully in order that we might ourselves live in chastity and also help and support others to do likewise.

The Seventh Commandment

"You shall not steal."

First, I can learn here that I must not take property belonging to my neighbors from them or possess it against their will, either in secret or openly. I must not be false or dishonest in business, service, or work, nor profit by fraud, but must support myself by the sweat of my brow and eat my bread in honor. Furthermore, I must see to it that in any of the above-named ways my neighbors are not defrauded, just as I wish for myself. I also learn in this commandment that God, in his fatherly solicitude, sets a protective hedge around my goods and solemnly prohibits anyone to steal from me. Where that is ignored, he has imposed a penalty and those in authority are ordered to punish the disobedient. Where that cannot be done, God himself metes out punishment and they become beggars in the end. As the proverb says, "Those who steal in their youth go begging in old age," or, "Stolen gain goes down the drain."

In addition I give thanks for his steadfast goodness in that he has given such excellent teachings, assurance, and protection to me and to all the world. If it were not for his protection, not a penny or a crumb of bread would be left in the house.

Third, I confess my sins and ingratitude in such instances where I have wronged, deprived, or cheated anyone in my life.

Fourth, I ask that he grant to me and all the world grace to learn from this commandment, to ponder it, and to become better people, so that there may be less theft, robbery, usury, cheating, and injustice and that the Judgment Day, for which all saints and the whole creation pray, Romans 8:20-23, shall soon bring this to an end. Amen.

The Eighth Commandment

"You shall not bear false witness against your neighbor." This teaches us, first of all, to be truthful to each other, to shun lies and calumnies, to be glad to speak well of each other, and to delight in hearing what is good about others. Thus a wall has been built around our good reputation and integrity to protect it against malicious gossip and deceitful tongues; God will not let those go unpunished, as he has said in the other commandments.

We owe him thanks both for the teachings and the protection which he has graciously provided for us.

Third, we confess and ask forgiveness that we have spent our lives in ingratitude and sin and have maligned our neighbor with false and wicked talk, though we owe him the same preservation of honor and integrity which we desire for ourselves.

Fourth, we ask for help from now on to keep the commandment and for a healing tongue.

The Ninth and Tenth Commandments

"You shall not covet your neighbor's house." You shall not covet your neighbor's wife, or his manservant, or his maidservant, or his cattle, or anything that is your neighbor's.

This teaches us first that we shall not dispossess our neighbors of their goods under pretense of legal claims, or lure away, alienate, or extort what is theirs but help them to keep what is theirs, just as we wish to be done for ourselves. It is also a protection against the subtleties and chicaneries of shrewd manipulators who will receive their punishment in the end. Second, we should render thanks to him. Third, we should repentantly and sorrowfully confess our sins. Fourth, we should ask for help and strength devoutly to keep such divine commandments.

These are the Ten Commandments in their fourfold aspect, namely, as a school text, song book, penitential book, and prayer book. They are intended to help the heart come to itself and grow zealous in prayer. Take care, however, not to undertake all of this or so much that one becomes weary in spirit. Likewise, a good prayer should not be lengthy or drawn out, but frequent and ardent. It is enough to consider one section or half a section which kindles a fire in the heart. This the Spirit will grant us and continually instruct us in when, by God's word, our hearts have been cleared and freed of outside thoughts and concerns.

I repeat here what I previously said in reference to the Lord's Prayer: if in the midst of such thoughts the Holy Spirit begins to preach in your heart with rich, enlightening thoughts, honor him by letting go of this written scheme; be still and listen to him who can do better than you can. Remember what he says and note it well and you will behold wondrous things in the law of God, as David says (Ps. 119:18).

Nothing can be said here about the part of faith and Holy Scriptures in prayer because there would be no end to what could be said. With practice one can take the Ten Commandments on one day, a psalm or chapter of Holy Scripture the next day, and use them as flint and steel to kindle a flame in the heart.

THE APOSTLES' CREED

If you have more time, or the inclination, you may treat the Creed in the same manner and make it into a garland of four strands. The Creed, however, consists of three main parts or articles, corresponding to the three Persons of the Divine Majesty, as it has been so divided in the Catechism and elsewhere.

The First Article

"I believe in God, the Father Almighty, creator of heaven and earth."

Here, first of all, a great light shines into your heart if you permit it to and teaches you in a few words what all the languages of the world and a multitude of books cannot describe or fathom in words, namely, who you are, whence you came, whence came heaven and earth. You are God's creation, his handiwork. That is, of yourself and in yourself you are nothing, can do nothing, know nothing, are capable of nothing. What were you a thousand years ago? What were heaven and earth before creation? Nothing, just as that which will never be created is nothing. But what you are, know, can do, and can achieve is God's creation, as you confess in the Creed by word of mouth. Therefore you have nothing to boast of before God except that you are nothing and he is your Creator who can annihilate you at any moment.

Reason knows nothing of such a light. Many great thinkers have sought to know what heaven and earth, people and animals are and have found no answer. But here it is declared and faith affirms that God has created everything out of nothing. Here is the soul's garden of pleasure, along whose paths we enjoy the works of God—but it would take too long to describe all that.

Furthermore, we should give thanks to God that in his kindness he has created us out of nothing and provides for our daily needs out of nothing—has made us to be such excellent beings with body and soul, intelligence, five senses, and has ordained us to be masters of earth, of fish, bird, and beast, etc. Here consider Genesis, chapters one to three.

Third, we should confess and lament our lack of faith and gratitude in failing to take this to heart, or to believe, ponder, and acknowledge it, and having been more stupid than unthinking beasts.

Fourth, we pray for a true and confident faith that sincerely esteems and trusts God to be our Creator, as this article declares.

The Second Article

"And in Jesus Christ, his only Son, our Lord. He was conceived by the power of the Holy Spirit and born of the virgin Mary. He suffered under Pontius Pilate, was crucified, died, and was buried. He descended into hell. On the third day he rose again. He ascended into heaven, and is seated at the right hand of the Father. He will come again to judge the living and the dead."

Again a great light shines forth and teaches us how Christ, God's Son, has redeemed us from death which, after the creation, had become our lot through Adam's fall and in which we would have perished eternally. Now think: just as in the first article you were to consider yourself one of God's creatures and not doubt it, now you must think of yourself as one of the redeemed and never doubt that. Emphasize one word above all others, for instance, Jesus Christ, *our* Lord. Likewise, suffered for *us*, died for *us*, arose for *us*. All this is ours and pertains to us; that *us* includes yourself, as the word of God declares.

Second, you must be sincerely grateful for such grace and rejoice in your salvation.

Third, you must sorrowfully lament and confess your wicked unbelief and mistrust of such a gift. Oh, what thoughts will come to mind—the idolatry you have practiced repeatedly, how much you have made of praying to the saints and of innumerable good works of yours which have opposed such salvation.

Fourth, pray now that God will preserve you from this time forward to the end in true and pure faith in Christ our Lord.

The Third Article

"I believe in the Holy Spirit, the holy catholic Church, the communion of saints, the forgiveness of sins, the resurrection of the body, and the life everlasting. Amen."

This is the third great light which teaches us where such a Creator and Redeemer may be found and plainly encountered in this world, and what this will all come to in the end. Much could be said about this, but here is a summary: Where the holy Christian church exists, there we can find God the Creator, God the Redeemer, God the Holy Spirit, that is, him who daily sanctifies us through the forgiveness of sins. The church exists where the word of God concerning such faith is rightly preached and confessed.

Again you have occasion here to ponder long about everything that the Holy Spirit accomplishes in the church every day.

Therefore be thankful that you have been called and have come into such a church.

Confess and lament your lack of faith and gratitude, that you have neglected all this, and pray for a true and steadfast faith that will remain and endure until you come to that place where all endures forever, that is, beyond the resurrection from the dead, in life eternal. Amen.

PRAYERS FOR ENLIGHTENMENT FROM GOD'S WORD

*Dear Lord Jesus Christ, prepare,
strengthen, and establish us
thoroughly in your eternal kingdom
with all the dimension of your wisdom
and knowledge.*

Prayers for Enlightenment from God's Word

We call upon God for grace: (1) To enable us to learn his Word well; (2) To live devoutly in accordance with it; (3) To die happy in believing it.

84.

Before Going to Church

Dear God, you do say through your beloved Son: Blessed are they who hear God's Word. O merciful and eternal God, it would be better for us gladly to call you blessed and to praise and thank you for having made yourself known to us miserable ones in such a friendly and fatherly way. You speak to us of the greatest and the highest things, which are eternal life and blessedness. You do not fail to call us graciously through your Son to hear your Word when he says: Blessed are they who hear God's Word and keep it. We are dust and ashes and stand in need of your word a thousand times more than you need hearers. O how inexpressibly wonderful and great are your goodness and patience! And how pitiful is the thanklessness and total blindness of those who not only fail to hear your word but also maliciously despise, persecute, and blaspheme it. O God, the Father of all poor, forlorn souls, grant all of us your grace and enlighten us with your truth. Praise, honor, and thanks be to you throughout eternity. Amen.

85.

While Entering Church

O God, the Father of all mercy, we sincerely thank you at all times that at the cost of your grace you have brought us to the treasure of your Word, in which we have the knowledge of your dear Son. This is a sure pledge to us of the life and salvation that will be ours in heaven and is prepared for all who remain in true faith and fervent love to the end. O merciful Father, we hope and pray that you will preserve us and make us perfect with all the elect and will keep us united in the mind and image of your dear Son, Jesus Christ, our Lord. Amen.

86.

After Attending Worship Services

O dear God, give us grace, that like Paul, David, and other saints we may highly prize our treasure, which is the same as theirs. Help us to cherish it above our possessions on earth and to thank you from the heart that you have honored us with it in preference to thousands of others. You could have let us go astray like those who know nothing of this treasure. You could have left us hardened like those who blaspheme and condemn our treasure. It is pure grace that you have placed us in your green pastures and have so richly provided us with the bread of heaven and the water of life. For these we owe you more than hearty thanks. Dear Lord Jesus Christ, prepare, strengthen, and establish us thoroughly in your eternal kingdom with all the dimension of your wisdom and knowledge. To you be praise and thanks in eternity. Amen.

87.

For a Right Understanding

Lord God, dear Father, through your Holy Spirit you have taught and enlightened the hearts of your believers. Through the same Spirit give us a right understanding, to be glad at all times in his comfort and power, through your Son, Jesus Christ, our Lord. Amen.

88.

Before the Sermon

Eternal God and Father of our Lord Jesus Christ, give us your Holy Spirit who writes the preached Word into our hearts. May we receive and believe it and be cheered and comforted by it in eternity. Glorify your Word in our hearts and make it so bright and warm that we may find pleasure in it, through your Holy Spirit think what is right, and by your power fulfill the Word, for the sake of Jesus Christ, your Son, our Lord. Amen.

89.

After the Sermon

Dear Lord Christ, you have enlightened my heart with your truth. Grant me your Spirit and the power to do and not to do whatever pleases your gracious will. Amen.

90.

Believing and Living the Word

O Father of all mercy, you have begun your work in us. Continue to fill us with all dimensions of wisdom and knowledge. May we be fully certain in our hearts and fully aware how the Spirit, who has raised up our Lord, also enlivens the faith within us with the same power and strength. Through him we have also risen from the dead by his mighty power, which works in us through your holy Word. Help us to grow in the knowledge of your dear Son, our Lord Jesus Christ, and to remain firm in confessing his blessed Word.

Give us the love to be agreed in mind and to serve one another in Christ. May we not be afraid of that which is disagreeable, nor of the rage of the flame-hurler whose weapon is almost extinguished. Dear Father, guard us so that his craftiness may not take the place of our pure faith. Grant that our cross and sufferings may direct us to a blessed and sure hope of the coming of our Savior Jesus Christ, for whom we wait each day. Amen.

91.

That Our Emptiness Be Filled

Look, Lord, an empty vessel that needs to be filled. My Lord, fill it. I am weak in the faith; strengthen me. I am cold in love; warm me and make me fervent, that my love may go out to my neighbor. I do not have a strong and firm faith. At times I doubt and am unable to trust you completely. O Lord, help me. Strengthen my faith and trust in you. I have insured all my treasure in your name. I am poor; you are rich and you did come to be merciful to the poor. I am a sinner; you are upright. With me there is an abundance of sin; with you a fullness of righteousness. Therefore I will remain with you, from whom I can receive but to whom I may not give. Amen.

92.

For a Daily Increase in Faith

O God, what would we be if you were to forsake us? What can we do if you withdraw your hand? What can we know if you do not enlighten? How quickly the educated become infants; the prudent, simple; the wise, fools! How terrifying you are in all your works and judgments! Let us walk in the light while we have light, so that we may not be caught in darkness. Many renounce their faith and become careless and weary in your grace. They are deceived by Satan into thinking they know everything and have no need. They feel satisfied and become slothful and ungrateful and are soon ruined. Therefore help us to remain in the fervor of faith, that we may daily increase in it through Jesus Christ, our real and only helper. Amen.

93.

For Preservation from Sin, Death, and Hell

O dreadful and severe Judge, how mysterious and terrible your judgments are! How sure and safe Pharaoh was before he perished in the Red Sea. Even his sense of security was God's real and stern judgment upon him. O God, so jealous are you of your Word that you have allowed it to cost the blood of your beloved Son. And yet, people smile as they hear it condemned and persecuted. Heavenly Father, your judgments are right. You are a witness to my fear that if this sacrilege does not soon end, you will take away your Word and will send our nation such blindness and so harden it that I shudder at the thought. Lord, heavenly Father, if we cannot help falling into other sins, at least preserve us from deserting you. Keep us near and in him, whom you have appointed to be Master over sin and innocence. Then surely all sin and death and hell cannot harm us. Amen.

94.

Saved Only by Grace

Dear Lord God, I cannot count the sins that I have done and still do. I have forgotten most of them and no longer feel my guilt. All that is in me and all power that is not grace is sin and is condemned. My works and my powers only make me despondent. I do not know what else to do but to hope and pray for your mercy. As grace and faith control me, I am devout through Christ. Where these fail me, I know and confess that nothing good is left in me. No matter how long I live, it will never be different. If I had the holiness of all monks, there would still be nothing good in what I think, speak, live, and do, if it did not have your divine grace and power. All my sins are forgiven out of pure grace. This is the joy and comfort which you gladly grant to me, a poor sinner. Amen.

95.

Before Confession and Absolution

Dear Lord God, that I am a sinner before you is as real as my conception, my birth, my nature, my thoughts, words, works, and my entire being are sinful. I am a corrupt tree and by nature a child of sin and wrath. As long as this nature remains with us we are sinners and must say: Forgive us our debts. So I confess what you command, in order that you may be just when you judge. Lord, I am an evil-doer and a sinner against your divine commandment. You help me, for I am helpless. Amen.

96.

For Triumph Over Sin

O Lord, I am your clay. You are my potter and skilled master. Because you pronounce me a sinner, I accept your word. I sincerely acknowledge and confess the godless condition which shows itself in my flesh and my entire nature. I do so that you may be glorified and I humiliated. As with all others, I am sin and death; you are life and righteousness. Together with all people I am the worst evil; you are and remain the highest good. I acknowledge and confess all this. I am led to this confession not by my reason, which would rather cover up and disguise this godless condition, but through your law and promises, I want your honor to stay and increase. Lord, I am your sin; your are my righteousness. Therefore I am glad and have victory without fear. For my sin cannot outweigh or overpower your righteousness. Neither will your righteousness permit me to be or remain a sinner. Your Spirit, O Lord, must make and keep me alive. Blessed are you, O faithful God, my merciful Redeemer. In you alone do I trust. Therefore I will not be baffled. Amen.

97.

Before Going to Sleep

My dear Father, I always confess and you can see that as I walk or stand, every particle of my inner and outer being, together with my body and soul, deserves hell and fire. When all is said and done, you, my Father, know that of my own accord there is not even a hair on my head, nor any other thing in me, that is good. Everything that belongs to me is hunted by the hated devil for the bottomless pit.

What can I say about it? In spite of who I am, I continue to pray to you, my dear Father. Do not stare and search me with your eyes, for I would be lost and destroyed, even if a hundred thousand worlds were mine! But I ask you to look at the faces of your dear Son, Jesus

Christ, your anointed one, my Mediator, High Priest, and Advocate; my Savior, Redeemer, and Benefactor. O my Father, be gracious and merciful for his sake, not mine.

Grant me a happy end and a glad resurrection, for the sake of your dear Son, Jesus Christ. Help my body in this world, and my soul in the world to come, because of the crimson blood which he has shed on the cross for the forgiveness of my sins, and because of my many sins which cannot be named, which because of your righteousness you will not cover. I pray you now, my Father, because of your infinite mercy permit the blood of Jesus Christ your Son to accomplish its purpose in me. It was willed by you from eternity that the shedding of the blood of Jesus Christ on the cross should pay for the forgiveness and remission of my sins.

So in whatever hour or moment by day or night you will come and knock to require my spirit which you have breathed into me, I pray you continually, dear Father, to permit this spirit, which is my soul, to be commended into your hands. I ask this because of the blood, the sufferings, and death of your dear Son, Jesus Christ, our Lord. Amen.

98.

Consecration

O Jesus Christ, I live to you; I die to you; living or dying, I am yours. Romans 14:7. Amen.

99.

For Forgiveness of Sins

Dear God, before you I confess that I am a great sinner. The Ten Commandments would drive me and commit me directly to hell. But your precious gospel teaches me to know and believe that out of love you have established a kingdom through Jesus Christ. In it you will be merciful and will help forlorn and condemned sinners. So I say my confession of faith and sin in one word: I am truly a sinner, but God is merciful to me. I am your enemy, but you are my friend. I deserve condemnation, yet I know that you do not want to condemn me.

You want me to be blessed and to inherit heaven. This is indeed your will. You have permitted this truth to be preached to me and have commanded me to believe it, for the sake of your Son whom you have given for me. Amen.

100.

For Help to Flee from Sin

Dear Lord Jesus Christ, I feel my sins. They bite and gnaw and frighten me. Where shall I go? I look to you, Lord Jesus, and believe in you. Although my faith is weak, I cling to you and am made sure, for you have promised: who believes in me shall have eternal life. Even if my conscience is troubled and my sins frighten me and make me tremble, you have still said: "My son, be of good cheer; your sins are forgiven you. I will raise you up on the last day, and you will have eternal life." I cannot help myself by my own strength. I come to you for help. Amen.

101.

Saved by the Good Shepherd

O God, these are your words: There is greater joy in heaven over one sinner who repents than over ninety-nine who do not repent. All the righteous and the angels will crush sin under their feet and will cover it. O my God, I feel my sins and am judged already. I am greatly in need of a shepherd to seek me. For this reason I rely completely on the gospel. O Lord, I know that I am a straying sheep and that you are the Shepherd and the One who seeks the lost. I want to hold to this assurance. In the mirror of your law I see that I am a scarred and lost sinner. Save me, O God, for the sake of your only begotten Son. Amen.

102.

For Comfort to Timid Consciences

My Lord Jesus Christ, although you are both God and King of heaven and earth, I need not be afraid of you. You are my companion and my brother, flesh and blood like me. That I am a sinner and you are holy causes me to give up. Yet if I had not been a sinner, you would not have suffered for me, and so I am comforted. Among your ancestors, of whom it was your will to be born, there were both the good and the bad. So we stand in your presence in order that you may comfort our timid and fearful consciences, and we may trust anew in you, knowing that you have also taken away our sin. You have indeed taken it away and have left us the Word that assures us of it. Praise to you in eternity. Amen.

103.

For Strengthened Faith

Almighty God, through the death of your Son you have destroyed sin and death. Through his resurrection you have restored innocence and eternal life. We who are delivered from the power of the devil may live in your kingdom. Give us grace that we may believe this with our whole heart. Enable us, always, to steadfastly praise and thank you in this faith, through your Son Jesus Christ, our Lord. Amen.

104.

For an Increase of Faith

O Lord, increase our faith. Gladly and truly I would think of you as my dearly beloved Father, and Christ as my brother. But alas, my deeds will not follow. Therefore, help my unbelief, so that I may accept your Word as truth and glorify your name. O Lord, end our captivity. Redeem us, for we are the firstborn of your new creation. As re-demption has been perfectly and sufficiently accomplished through

Christ, so may we fully and truly know and accept it. As by your mighty hand the sea was dried up by the parching wind, so let everything of our remaining bondage vanish. Amen.

105.

For a Clean Heart and a Firm Faith

I thank you, my dear God, that I have learned not to begin faith by my own efforts, nor attempt to destroy my sin with my own repentance. I might do this before other people and be acceptable to the world and its judges. But with you, O God, there is an eternal wrath which I cannot satisfy, and before it I would despair. Therefore I thank you that Another has seized and carried my sins and has made atonement for them. With joy I wish to believe this. It seems so very right and comforting to me. But I cannot believe it by myself, and I find no power in me to convince myself. I cannot comprehend it as I ought. Lord, lead me, help me. Give me the power and gift to believe. I plead, as did David: "Create in me a clean heart, O God, and put a new and right spirit within me." I am unable to create a new and clean heart: It is your work and creation. I cannot create the sun and mon and make them rise and shine brightly in the heavens any more than I can make the heart clean and give myself a right spirit, a strong and firm frame of mind that is unbending and unwavering and that will not doubt or mistrust your Word. Help us daily to increase in faith. Though the world should topple and all conspire against us, and though the devil were to destroy every creature, grant that I may not fall. By your divine help let me remain in the Gospel. Amen.

106.

Longing for the Good Shepherd

My Lord Jesus Christ, you are indeed the only Shepherd, and I, sorry to say, am the lost and straying sheep. I an anxious and afraid. Gladly would I be devout and cling to you, my gracious God, and so have peace in my heart. I learn that you are as anxious for me as I am for you. I am eager to know how I can come to you for help. Anxiously you desire above all else to bring me back to yourself again. Then come to me. Seek and find me. Help me also to come to you and praise and honor you forever. Amen.

107.

For Acceptance of Blessings

O merciful God, what a kind and gracious Father you are, to deal so sincerely and paternally with us poor and judged sinners. You did release your most precious possession, your Son, Jesus Christ, into the jaws of death and the devil. You did require that he should descend into the deep and again ascend on high and conquer the captivity which has held us all in slavery. Through this we are your dear children, his brothers and sisters, and inheritors of all his eternal, heavenly blessings. Give us your Holy Spirit so that he may preserve us to the end in faith. Grant your grace that youth and those unborn, the weak in faith and those not properly instructed, may get and keep a right understanding in the doctrine of becoming fellow citizens with the angels. So highly privileged are we who believe in Christ. Amen.

108.

Thanksgiving for Baptism

I thank, praise, and glorify you, my Lord Christ, with heart and voice before the world that you are merciful to me and do help me. This I have received in baptism, that you and none other shall be my Lord and God. Amen.

109.

Prayer for a Child to be Baptized

Dear God, you will not only rescue this child from the power of the devil, but you will also strengthen it, that the child may boldly resist the devil in life and in death. Amen.

110.

Before Communion

My Lord Christ, I have fallen, I would gladly be strong. For this purpose you have instituted the sacrament, that with it we may rekindle and strengthen our faith and be helped. Therefore I am to receive it. Behold, Lord, it is your word. My weakness and failings are known to you. You, yourself, have said: "Come to me, all you that are weary and are carrying heavy burdens and I will give you rest" (Matt. 11:28). I now come to be helped. Amen.

111.

While Communing

Lord, it is true that I am not worthy that you should come under my roof. Yet I am in need and desire your help and grace. So I come with no other plea except that I have heard the gracious invitation to come to your altar. I am unworthy, but you have assured me I shall have forgiveness of all sins through your body and blood which I eat and drink in this sacrament. Amen, dear Lord; your Word is true. I do not doubt it. Let happen to me whatever you say. Amen.

112.

After Communion

We thank you, almighty Lord God, that you have refreshed us with this precious gift, and we ask for your mercy that you would let it nurture in us strong faith toward you and intensive love among us all, through Jesus Christ, your Son our Lord. Amen.

113.

For a Better Life

Lord Jesus Christ, I receive your Supper, and yet I go on without bearing fruit as before. I regret that I have received this great treasure only to let it be dormant within me. Since you have given this blessing to me, may it so change my life that I will show kindness to my neighbors. Help us by your Holy Spirit to thank you from the heart for this sacrament and to use it worthily to our salvation. Amen.

114.

Thanksgiving for Benefits in the Sacraments

O my God, I am a sinner, and yet I am not a sinner. Alone and apart from Christ, I am a sinner. But in my Lord Jesus Christ and with him, I am no sinner. I firmly believe that he has destroyed all my sins with his precious blood. The sign of this is that I am baptized, cleansed by God's word, and declared absolved and freed from all my sins. In the sacrament of the true body and blood of my Lord Jesus Christ I have received as a sure sign of grace the forgiveness of sins. This he has won and accomplished for me by the shedding of his precious blood. For this I thank him in eternity. Amen.

115.

For Preservation of the Church

O Lord, although you are rightfully angry with us on account of our sins, you have never deserted the human race. You have always preserved a church for yourself among those who have looked to you for all blessings and comfort. You have been their dwelling and their refuge. Dear God, keep us and your little flock, that we may escape the bitter wrath. May you find us among those who honor and serve Christ, gladly waiting for the judgment with the blessed at his right hand. Amen.

116.

For Devout Teachers of the Gospel

Dear Lord God, bring blessedness and salvation to the holy church which is the kingdom of Christ. Send us faithful and God-fearing teachers who will reveal your name to the world and who proclaim that you are gracious and merciful, forgiving us our sins for the sake of your Son. He will grant us eternal life in order that all people may rely on your grace and mercy, call upon you, and give you praise and thanks. Abolish all human doctrines and let Christ alone be our King, ruling through his gospel and making us his servants (John 13:12-16). Amen.

117.

For Protection of the Church

Almighty and everlasting Father of our Lord and Savior Jesus Christ, we see and feel how your church is doing in this world. We see its status and how it is annoyed in so many ways by the world and the devil. So we pray to you for the sake of your only begotten Son. First, comfort and strengthen our hearts by your Holy Spirit, so that we may not be overwhelmed by so many dangers. Also we pray that you will not only halt the purposes and plans of the enemies but will truly and marvelously help prove to the whole world that you care for the church. Rule, protect, and deliver it, ever living and reigning eternal God, God the Father, God the Son, and God the Holy Spirit. Amen.

118.

For Extension of the Church

Dear God, we are truly tortured by sin and surrounded by death. We have become the shameful images of the devil. Restore again to us your work which is righteous and gives life. Deliver us from the works of the devil, by which he has cast us from life into death. Dear son of God, Jesus Christ, you came to earth to destroy his works. You did abolish death and bring life and immortality to light. Give us your grace that we may continually extend your kingdom, and may diminish and destroy the devil's kingdom. Send laborers into your harvest who with angels will take away the offences now present and so numerous in your kingdom on earth. Amen.

119.

For the Lord to Punish False Prophets

Oh Lord, you are a God of vengeance. You alone reward and punish all wickedness. Oh break forth as the day. Reveal yourself that everyone may see you. Tyrants and false prophets have come out into the open, have gained the upper hand, and exult in their victory. But you remain silent and hide yourself, as though you were buried and would come no more, for you do not resist and punish this wickedness. Therefore we beseech you again, arise. Show your face and let it appear against the wicked. You are to punish. If it is possible for some who persecute the gospel to be converted, we heartily desire it and pray for it. We fear if it is out of the question, for we have so long and ardently admonished and pleaded with them. Still they rave against the truth. We commit them to your judgment, for it is righteous. Amen.

PRAYERS FOR A CHRISTIAN LIFE

*Dear Father in heaven, for the
sake of your dear Son Jesus
Christ grant us your Holy Spirit, that
we may be true learners of
Christ, and therefore acquire a heart
with a never-ceasing fountain
of love.*

PRAYERS FOR A CHRISTIAN LIFE

120.

For God to Nurture and Help Us

Dear God and Father, we thank you for your infinite goodness and love to us. You do continually keep us in your word, in faith, and in prayer. By this we know how to walk before you in humility and in fear. By this we are not proud of our own wisdom, righteousness, skill, and strength, but glory alone in your power. You are strong when we are weak, and through our weakness you win daily and gain the victory. We pray for you to so nurture us that we may be to you as beautiful pleasure gardens so that many people may enjoy our fruits and be attracted through us to all godliness. Write into our hearts, by your Holy Spirit, whatever is abundantly found in Scripture. Let us constantly keep it in mind, and permit it to become far more precious to us than our own life and all else that we cherish on earth. Help us to live and act accordingly. To you be praise and thanks in eternity. Amen.

121.

For Help in Keeping the Commandments

Lord God, I have indeed transgressed your commandments. I have been impatient in reverses and trials. I am unsympathetic and unmerciful. I do not help my neighbor. I am unable to resist sin. I do not tire of doing wrong. Dear Lord, pour out your grace to me and give me your Holy Spirit so that I may be obedient and keep each of your commandments. Help me to be at odds with the world and to give my heart and soul to you. Amen.

122.

For Lasting Peace

Dear God, give us peaceful hearts and a right courage in the confusion and strife against the devil. And so may we not only endure and finally triumph, but also have peace in the midst of the struggle. May we praise and thank you and not complain or become impatient against your divine will. Let peace win the victory in our hearts, that we may never through impatience initiate anything against you, our God, or our neighbors. May we remain quiet and peaceable toward God and toward other people, both inwardly and outwardly, until the final and eternal peace shall come. Amen.

123.

For the Redeemed to Please God

Lord, we have prayed for your work. For we have no part in it. Work so we may receive your grace and blessing. For only through your work you do reveal yourself and make us blessed. It is accomplished in our redemption from the misery of sin and eternal death, which Satan has brought upon all of us through Adam. We who are justified by it do follow this work of yours with our work in holiness and obedience in your word. This is acceptable and pleasing to you, though it comes from your grace and proceeds from your work. Our Lord and God, be gracious to us so that we who are reconciled to you through the death of your Son may please you. Amen.

124.

For love toward others

Dear Father in heaven, for the sake of your dear Son Jesus Christ grant us your Holy Spirit, that we may be true learners of Christ, and therefore acquire a heart with a never-ceasing fountain of love. Amen.

125.

For Christlike Service to Neighbors

Lord, I fail, for you give yourself so richly and abundantly to me, and I cannot do the same to my neighbor. I regret this before you and pray that I may become so rich and so strong that I may do to my neighbor as you do to me. Dear God, I have been wronged. Why? I do not deserve it of this person. But I must remember and understand who I am to you. There is a long complaint against me, proving that I am ten times worse and have sinned a thousand times more against you than my neighbor has against me. Therefore I must agree with your wish by sincerely praying: O Lord, forgive, and I will also forgive. Amen.

126.

For a More Charitable Feeling Toward Neighbors

My Lord Jesus Christ, my neighbor has injured me, hurt my honor by talking about me, and interfered with my rights. I cannot tolerate this, and I wish to avoid any contact. O God, hear my complaint. I would gladly feel kindly toward my neighbor, but I cannot. How totally cold and insensible I am. O Lord, I am helpless and forsaken. If you change me, I will be sincere. O dear God, change my by your grace, or I must remain as I am. Amen.

127.

For Faith to Overcome Trials

O Father and God of all comfort, through your word and Holy Spirit grant us a firm, glad, and grateful faith. By it may we easily overcome this and every other trial, and at length realize that what your dear Son Jesus Christ himself says is true: "But take courage; I have conquered the world" (John 16:33). Amen.

128.

For Pardon and Deliverance from Sin

O God, where is there another like you? You forgive sin and forgive the iniquity of the lowest of your people. You do not stay angry forever, for you are merciful and you pardon our transgressions and cast all our sins into the deep sea. Do continue forever to be merciful, so that we may walk in the light of your Word and escape every trap of Satan and of the world, through Jesus Christ, your Son, our Redeemer. Amen.

129.

For Help with Responsibilities

Heavenly Father, you are indeed my Lord and God. You have created me out of nothing and have also redeemed me through your Son. Now you have placed special responsibility upon me. Here my will is not respected, and there is so much that bothers and worries me, for which I can find neither help nor counsel by myself. Therefore let these cares become yours. Grant me your help and counsel. Be all things to me in this place. Amen.

130.

Submission to Suffering

Dear God, I am your creature. You have sent me a cross and suffering, saying to me: Suffer a little for my sake and I will reward you well. Dear God, because it is your will I will gladly suffer. Amen.

131.

Rebuked for Our Sins

Dear Father, it is easy for you to reprimand and punish. Alas, I have deserved it. Nevertheless, let it be a Father's rod, as you chastise all your children whom you love. Those whom you do not rebuke for their sins are not children but are abandoned. But merciful Father, reprove us in such a way that your Father's heart will not turn from us. So may we praise you forever in this world and the next. Amen.

132.

For an End to Suffering

Dear God, you have overwhelmed us with many setbacks and have enabled us clearly to see your wrath. Stop afflicting us now, dear God, for you have mortified us long enough and sufficiently weighed and burdened and humiliated us. Graciously face us again and assure us how gentle and merciful you are, that we may comfort and quiet our troubled hearts. Amen.

133.

For Realization of the Purpose of Suffering

O Father of all mercy and God of all comfort, strengthen and uphold me by your Spirit. You command that we should wait on him until the reason for our trials shall appear. For you do not for your own pleasure permit us to be tortured and grieved. In fact, you do not permit any evil to be done unless you can make it serve a good purpose. You see my distress and weakness. Therefore you will help and deliver me. Amen.

134.

Under Great Trials and Persecution
(At the Diet in Worms, April 18, 1521)

Almighty and eternal God, what a strange cause this is! How it loosens peoples' tongues! How small and insignificant is their trust in you! How weak and tender is the flesh, and how powerful and busy is the devil, with the help of his apostles and the worldly wise! How quickly the world withdraws help, does an about-face, pursues the easy way, and speeds on the broad road to hell where the godless belong. It sees only what is brilliant and powerful, great, mighty, and respected! If I should turn my eyes to it, I would be done for.

Oh God, Oh God, Oh my God, Oh my God, stand by me against all the wisdom and reason of the world. Do it. You alone must do it. It is not really my concern; it is yours. Alone I have nothing to do with these great lords of the world. I want good and quiet days, undisturbed. But it is your cause; it is righteous and eternal. Stand by me. Oh true and eternal God. I do no rely on human counsel, for it would be in vain. All that is carnal and tastes carnal falters.

O God, O God, do you not hear me, my God? Are you dead? No, you cannot die; you are only hiding. Have you called me to this place? I ask you so that I may be sure. God, grant it! Never in my life had I thought to oppose such great rulers and never had I set out to do it.

O God, stand by me in the name of your dear Son Jesus Christ who shall be my Protector and Defender, even my mighty Fortress, through the power and help of your Holy Spirit.

Lord, where are you? Come, come, I am ready like a patient lamb to lay down my life for this cause. It is your cause and it is righteous. I will not separate myself from you forever. Be it resolved in your name that the world cannot force me to act against my conscience, even if I had still more devils, and if my body which is first of all your creation should have to perish. So your Word and Spirit come to my rescue even if only for the body. And my soul is yours. It belongs to you, and may it remain with you forever. Amen. So help me. Amen.

135.

Thanks for the Protection of the Angels

Dear heavenly Father, I thank and praise you that although I am weak, and with the help of a hundred thousand like me I could not resist one devil, yet by the help of your holy angels I am able to oppose them all. And though I do not have so much as a tiny drop of wisdom, and the wicked and deceptive enemy has an oceanful, yet he shall not know how or be able to harm me.

My merciful God and Father of my Lord Jesus Christ, I owe thanks to you alone for this blessing. This is your glory that you so declare your honor, wisdom, and might in shame, foolishness, and weakness. As you enable us through your beloved angels to smite the devil, you alone shall have the honor of being a wise, mighty, and gracious God. Dear God, help us to do this. Amen.

136.

For Uplifting

Dear Lord God, give me your grace that I may rightly understand your Word, and more than that, do it. O most blessed Lord Jesus

Christ, see to it that my search after knowledge leads me to glorify you alone. If not, let me not know a single letter. Give only what I, a poor sinner, need to glorify you. Amen.

137.

Prayer of a Young Preacher

Dear God, I have begun to preach, and to teach the people. It is hard. If it offends here and there, may no harm be done. Since you have commanded me to preach your Word, I will not stop. If it fails, it fails for you. If it succeeds, it succeeds for you and me. Amen.

138.

For God's Guidance for a Pastor

You know how unworthy I am to fill so great and important an office. Were it not for your counsel, I would have utterly failed long ago. Therefore I call upon you for guidance. Gladly will I give my heart and voice to this work. I want to teach the people. I want always to seek and study in your Word, and eagerly to meditate upon it. Use me as your instrument. Lord, do not forsake me. If I were alone, I would ruin everything. Amen.

139.

Relying Solely on God's Word

Dear heavenly Father, say something. I will gladly remain silent and be a child and learner. If I should rule the church with my own knowledge, wisdom, and understanding, I would have been sunk long ago. Therefore, dear God, you guide and direct it. I will gladly forsake my point of view and understanding and let you rule alone through your Word. Amen.

140.

Pastor as a Guide to Worship

I do not worship my pastor, but he tells me of a Lord whose name is Christ, and makes him known to me. I will be attentive to listen to his words as long as he leads me to this Master and Teacher who is the Son of God. Amen.

141.

Giving God the Glory

Lord, what you do not do remains undone. If you will not help, I shall gladly surrender. The cause is not mine. I will happily be your mask and disguise if only you will do the work. Amen.

142.

For Divine Help to Convince Hearers

O God, you see that at times they ridicule, blaspheme, and condemn me on account of your Word. There is no one to praise me. Uphold me and prove that I teach the truth. Enable me, like your dear Son, to say to you: Glorify me that I may also glorify you. Grant me your Spirit. Do signs and wonders in order that my teaching may be confirmed. May I glorify you and preach that you are my true God and Father. Then shall they believe me and be glorified with me. Amen.

143.

For Orderliness among Rulers

Dear Lord God, guide the hearts of our leaders to your praise and glory, and to the welfare of the land. Enlighten all who are in authority and move them to do what is right. Preserve your people, your judgment, your righteousness, and all administration of justice in this nation and throughout the world. Then good order will prevail.

May peace in the world not b e troubled by rebellion and treason. May proper discipline and respect not be disregarded or violated by unfaithfulness and other evil. Amen.

144.

For Uprightness and Usefulness of Rulers

O Father of all grace, preserve our rulers in their knowledge of you and your pure word. May they know themselves to be in the midst of wolves, and surely not altogether free from dangerous influence, especially in these evil and perilous times. Guard them against all abuse of their authority. Since they have the means to assist many sad, forsaken, and sinning souls, send your Spirit upon them that they may accomplish many great things to the praise and glory of your word. Amen.

145.

For Rulers

May we commend to your all who rule and have authority through-out all Christendom. Enlighten their hearts by your Word and your Holy Spirit, so that your Word and glory may be upheld by them and not hindered. And so may we lead a quiet and peaceable life among them by being godly and honest. Amen.

146.

For Success Over Enemies

Also give our rulers success over enemies. Remember your grace and mercy and preserve us from falling into the hands of any tyrant. Also guard our rulers against the devil and evil doctrine. Amen.

147.

A Ruler's Prayer for a Successful Administration

Oh God, Creator and Ruler of all things, lover of my soul, teach me how to protect the responsibility entrusted to me. Show me where I may find your help to preside faithfully and well over these people. I am ruling in the world as one in a dark night and a thick mist, but you dwell in the bright midday. If only I could also rule in the high noon of peace. Let me not lose heart or sink down under great hardships. Rule and guide me. Grant that I may not rely on my own wisdom. Favor us with blessed progress, success, and a quiet and peaceful government. Amen.

148.

For Help to Rule

Help me, dear God, so to rule my life that I may rule my land and people according to your command, maintaining your honor. Amen.

149.

For Divine Aid to Disregard Self and to Consider the Common Welfare

My Lord and God, you know I would rather be alone at home without a scepter, without power, silver, gold, fanfare, and popularity. But you wish for me to have this office, for you have elected me instead of others. Therefore I surrender to your will. Help me to rule, not according to my desires and pleasures, but for the furtherance of the common welfare. Amen.

150.

Prayer of a Soldier

Dear God, you see that I must go to war. I would surely rather keep out of it. I do not rely and trust in the righteous cause, but upon your grace and mercy. I will not wage war against you, neither will I be in an army that robs God of the things that are God's. O heavenly Father, here I am employed as you will in this work and service of my rulers. My first loyalty is to you; then to them, for your sake.

I have learned through your gracious Word that our works cannot help us and that no one is saved by being a warrior. I will in no way rely on my obedience and work as a soldier. But I will sincerely do this work as a service to your will.

Enable me to believe with all my heart that only the innocent blood of your dear Son, my Lord Jesus Christ, obediently shed for me according to your gracious will can redeem and save me. In this faith I will stay here, wage war, do all that has to do with war, and if need be, die. Dear God and Father, preserve and strengthen this faith in me through your Holy Spirit. Amen. I commend my body and soul into your hands. Amen.

151.

For Marriage

Dear God, I learn of you that marriage was instituted by you, and it is pleasing to you. Therefore I yield to your word. I shall be reconciled to whatever you permit to take place in this estate. Amen.

152.

For God's Guidance in Finding a Devout Husband or Wife

Dear God, you did institute marriage. Give me, your imperfect child, a devout wife (husband), so that I may live honestly and peaceably in true love, and that my will may be hers (his) and hers (his) will be mine. Choose for me one with whom I may serve you, and by faith and prayer overcome any trials of married life. Amen.

153.

For Help to Meet Parental Responsibilities

O Lord Jesus Christ, you have opened my eyes for me to see how through your death you have redeemed me from sin, and through your resurrection have made me an heir of heaven and eternal life. Now, dear Lord, I thank you for these great and unspeakable gifts. I will in turn gladly do what you require of me. You have commanded me to serve my wife (husband) faithfully, and to bear the responsibilities of family life diligently and submissively. I will gladly do this. You have made me father (mother) of a family. Dear Lord, make me a devout parent. Help me to discharge my parental duties with heart and soul. I would rather lose my life than disobey you by offending my children and members of my household or by failing to guide them faithfully. You will not permit this ordinance and blessing of yours to be disturbed or destroyed, but will graciously protect it through Jesus Christ our Lord. Amen.

154.

Entrusting a Child to God

Dear Father, your punishment is severe, but I am confident that you remain a loving Father. Dear Lord and Savior, Jesus Christ, you have been an example for all our sufferings. So impress yourself upon our hearts, and comfort us, that we may bring to you the sacrifices of our sorrowing spirits. With wailing hearts may we entrust our child to you, as Abraham entrusted his son Isaac. Amen.

155.

Requesting God to Become Head of the Family

Dear God, you have given to me my wife, children, house, and property. I receive these as you desire, and will care for them for your sake. Therefore I will do as much as possible that all may go well. If my plans do not all succeed, I will learn to be patient and let what cannot be changed take its course. If I do well I will give God the glory. I will say, O Lord, it is not my work or effort but your gift and providence. Take my place and be the head of the family. I will yield humbly and be obedient to you. Amen.

156.

Prayer of a Servant

Dear Lord God, I thank you that you have led me into this place and service. In it I know I serve and please you more than all nuns and monks who have no commandment for their service. But I have God's precept in the Fourth Commandment that I shall honor father and mother and serve master and servant with diligence and faithfulness, and assist them in keeping house. I will for their sakes willingly do what I must to please master and servant. I will be and not be as they desire. What does it matter if I am sometimes rebuked, so long as I am sure that my occupation is an approved life and service to you. My Lord and Redeemer, Jesus Christ, did himself attend a marriage and graced it with his presence and his service to his mother. Should not I also gladly do and give something to the honor and service of this holy estate? I will not object to being a dog in your house, so that I may at least eat the crumbs that fall from the table. You owe me positively nothing. I depend on your grace and mercy. Amen.

157.

For Blessings and Protection

Dear Father, give us our daily bread, good seasons, and health. Protect us from war, disease, and drought. If you would tempt me a bit by withholding your blessings for a while, then your will be done. If my time is up and my hour has come, deliver me from all evil. If not, give me strength and patience. Amen.

158.

Relying on God

Lord, I know that I cannot produce or preserve for myself even a piece of daily bread. Nor can I guard myself against any need or misfortune. Therefore I will pray as you order, and I hope to receive as you promise, for you take my need to heart and help before I even think of asking. If I please you, let it happen; if I do not, let it not happen. Amen.

159.

For Protection and Right Use of the Harvest

Dear Lord, graciously protect the crops in the fields. Cleanse the air; give refreshing rain and favorable weather that there may be a good harvest. Preserve the fruits from being polluted, so that the people and animals that eat and drink them may be protected from epidemic, fever, and other diseases. If you permit the forces of evil to contaminate the air and its fruits, the corn and the wine, then people will eat and drink sickness and death with their own food. Therefore, dear God, bless your gifts so that they may be wholesome and delightful to us. May we not use them to injure the soul or to increase sin, intemperance, and idleness. From these come unchastity, adultery, cursing, swearing, murder, war, and all misery. But give us grace to use your gifts to the saving of our souls and to the betterment of our lives. Thus may the fruits of the earth serve to maintain and improve the health of both body and soul. Amen.

160.

For the Best Use of Our Means

O Lord, come to me and use my bread, silver, and gold. How very well they are spent if I spend them in your service. Amen.

161.

The Lord Can and Will Provide for the Body

Dear God, why should I be anxious and worry about my body and its food? How do you raise up the grain on the field and all the fruits? The world with all its wisdom and power is not able to make a stalk, a tiny leaf, or a flower. In you I have a Lord who can multiply one loaf as much as you please, without the aid of a farmer, a miller, or a baker. As you do this day by day, why should I worry whether you can or will supply my bodily needs!

162.

I Shall Not Want

Dear Lord, I know that you own even more and have more in storage than you have given away. In you I shall not want. If need be, the heavens indeed would pour down a supply for our need. You will never fail me. You make me rich. If I have you, I have all I want. Amen.

163.

For True Preaching and Right Living

Almighty and everlasting God, we pray in the name of your dear Son, our Lord Jesus Christ. First, send a spiritual kingdom and a blessed gospel ministry. Give us devout and faithful preachers who communicate the wealth of your divine Word in truth and clarity. Graciously guard us against divisions and heresies. Do not focus on our ingratitude, by which we have long deserved that you take your word away from us. Do not punish us as severely as we deserve. Again we ask you to give us thankful hearts that we may love your holy Word, prize it highly, hear it reverently, and improve our lives accordingly. And so may we not only understand your Word rightly but also meet its demands by our deeds. May we live in accordance with it and day by day increase in good works. Thereby may your name be hallowed, your kingdom come, and your will be done. Amen.

164.

For Good Government

We pray especially for the government under whose care and protection you have called us. Bless it with success and prosperity. May the word of God, decency, and all honesty be advanced; may all of the offense of which there is so much be prevented; and may the common welfare be properly and peaceably provided. Make us obedient and devout. Amen.

165.

Commending All to the Lord

Permit the wife and child, with the sick and all afflicted in body and soul, to be commended to you. For these and all other needs, and for myself, I pray the Lord's Prayer: Our Father in heaven, hallowed be your name, your kingdom come, your will be done, on earth as in heaven. Give us today our daily bread. Forgive us our sins as we forgive those who sin against us. Save us from the time of trial and deliver us from evil. For the kingdom, the power, and the glory are yours, now and forever. Amen.   .

166.

Amen

Dear God, I know that my prayer spoken in the name of your dear Son, Jesus Christ, is indeed pleasing to you. It will most surely be heard. Amen. Amen.

PRAYERS WHEN DEATH DRAWS NEAR

*Grant that the glad and blessed
day of our redemption and
glorification may come soon, and that
we may realize it as we now hear
and believe your word.*

PRAYERS WHEN DEATH DRAWS NEAR

167.

Humbly Submitting to God

My dear God, if you want this to be the hour of death, let your will be done. Lord God, you are most precious to me. You know how gladly I would have shed my blood for the sake of your Word, but I may not deserve this honor. Your will be done. If it is your will, I shall die gladly. Only let your holy name be praised and glorified by my sufferings and death. If it were possible, dear God, I would live longer for the cause of your blessed and chosen people. But if the hour has come, then have your way. You are the Lord of life and death. Amen.

168.

For Confusion of God's Enemies

My Lord and God, you have led me to this cause. You know it is your Word and truth. Do not give heart and courage to your enemies, lest they ask proudly: Now where is your God? But glorify your name before your enemies. Confuse those who oppose your blessed and wholesome Word. Amen.

169.

For Comfort of Holy Spirit in the Hour of Death

My dearest Lord Jesus Christ, you have graciously told me about your holy name. You know that I believe in you, the Father, the Son, the Holy Spirit, the only true God. You are the Mediator and Savior who has shed precious blood for us sinners. Support me in this hour. Comfort me with your Holy Spirit. Lord, you know of the many whom you permitted to shed their own blood for professing the Gospel. I did hope it would be my privilege to shed my blood for the sake of your holy name, but I am not worthy of it. Your will be done. Amen.

170.

Accepting God's Gracious Invitation

Lord, you know that the devil has fought me in many ways. He would have destroyed my body through tyrants, kings, and rulers, and would have destroyed my soul with his weapons and terrible temptations. Until this moment you have wonderfully preserved me against all their rage and anger and wrath. If it be your will, dear Lord, continue to preserve me. Most gracious God, you are indeed a God of the weak and the sinful. They feel their need and anxiety, and from the heart they desire your grace, comfort, and help. They have the promise of your Word: "Come to me, all you that are weary and carry heavy burdens." Lord, I am in great trouble and distress. I accept the invitation to come. Help me because of your mercy and truth. Amen.

171.

Asking for the Best Gifts

O my dear Lord Jesus Christ, you have said: Ask, and it will be given you; search, and you will find; knock, and the door will be opened for you (Matt. 7:7). In keeping with this promise, give to me, Lord. I ask for neither gold nor silver, but for a strong and firm faith. While I search, let me find not lust and pleasure of the world, but comfort and refreshment through your blessed and healing Word. Open to me, while I knock. I desire nothing that the world cherishes, for by it I would not be uplifted even for so much as the breadth of a hair. Grant me your Holy Spirit, who enlightens my heart, and comforts and strengthens me in my cares and trials. He secures my right faith and trust in your grace to the very end. Amen.

172.

That All Divine Gifts Be Used to Praise God

O most precious God and Father, in preference to thousands of others you have given me so many priceless gifts. If it is your will, I would gladly use these gifts to serve your little flock. Let your divine and fatherly will be done, so that whether I live or die, your name may be praised through me. Amen.

173.

Commending the Soul to God

O heavenly Father, God and Father of my Lord Jesus Christ and God of all comfort, I thank you for revealing to me your dear Son, Jesus Christ, whom I believe. Him I have known and preached. Him I have loved and praised. Him heretics and all godless people do blaspheme and persecute. I pray, Lord Jesus, let my soul please you. O heavenly Father, although I must be separated from this body, I know I will remain with you forever. No one can pluck me from your hands. Amen.

174.

On Day of Luther's Death, Feb. 18, 1546

Father, into your hands I commend my spirit. You have redeemed me, faithful God. Amen.

175.

Absolved and Freed from Sin

Merciful God, be gracious to me. I an a sinful person and deserve nothing but your disapproval. Yet, regardless of my past life, I know for sure that I am baptized and am made a Christian for the forgiveness of sins. I know without doubt that my Lord Christ was born, suffered, died, and rose for me. He gave his body and blood for the nourishment of the soul and the strengthening of faith. Therefore I am absolved and freed in the name and the power of Christ.

176.

Blessed Assurance

Dear Lord, you know that I am a poor sinner; through your dear Son you have shown yourself to be gracious to me. You forgive my sins and do not hold your anger and condemnation. You want me to believe beyond all doubt. I rely on this assurance and I would gladly leave this life in it. Amen.

177.

The Only Safe Refuge

Lord, I know no one in heaven or earth who gives me the same assurance as you do through Jesus Christ. Nor do I have it in all friends, works, and honors. Lord, I have no refuge except in the affection which is now your Son's. Without this hope I would be lost. Amen.

178.

Relying on Christ's Merits While Dying

Dear Lord Christ, though I do not do your law, have sin, and fear death and hell, yet I know from the gospel that by faith all your merits are mine. I am sure of this, for you would not deceive me. You will surely keep your promise. As a sign of this I have received baptism and rely on it. Dear Father, if it please you, I would gladly die, for you are mine, dear Lord. Death cannot harm me, for it is swallowed up in victory. Praise be to you, Lord God, for you have given us the victory through our Lord Jesus Christ. Amen.

Very truly, I tell you, whoever keeps my word (which means, if he firmly believes in his heart that with my sufferings and death, and with my crimson blood shed on the tree of the cross, I have submerged, drowned, strangled and destroyed that person's sins), will never see death (John 8:51). Whether I am asleep or awake, eat or drink, stand or move, I continually await the sound of the last trumpet, when the dead who have fallen asleep in Jesus will come forth from the graves, and all will receive their reward from the Judge whom no one can deceive.

179.

Trusting in God for Deliverance

O Lord God, I am weak and fearful. I flee evil and do all I can to guard myself against it. Nevertheless, I am in your hands as I face this evil and every other evil that may overtake me. To flee is not enough, for evil and misery are everywhere. The devil, who has been murdering since the beginning, tries to bring misery, and he never rests nor sleeps. Now you have confined me to this place. Your will be done, for I am your poor creature. You are able to deliver me in this extreme danger as easily as though it were but fire, water, thirst, or any other peril. Amen.

180.

A Dying Father Commends His Family to God

My dearest God, I thank you from the heart for your will that I should be poor while on earth. For this reason I cannot leave to my wife and children a house or land or money or goods or property. As you have given my family to me I give them again to you, my rich and faithful God. O Father of the orphans and judge of the widows, support and teach and keep them as you have kept me. Amen.

181.

Comforting Assurances of Baptism When Dying

Dear God, I know that though I have done my best, I am still to blame. Yet I am comforted, for you have died for me and covered me with blood from your holy wounds. I am surely baptized in you and have heard the word through which you have called me, have commanded me to believe, and have assured me grace and life. With these blessings I will gladly go ahead, not anxious and hesitating and asking in doubt and fear. Who knows what judgment God in heaven will hold against me? I now live in the assurance of the gracious decree which God in heaven has given against the curse of the law: Everyone who believes in the Son of Man has eternal life. Amen.

182.

For Final Redemption

Lord Jesus Christ, hurry. Do not delay in bringing the blessed day when the hope of happy redemption will be fulfilled. For this reason you have asked us to pray: Your kingdom come. Since you have so commanded us to pray, give us grace and help to pray diligently, firmly believing that we shall finally come to such glory. Continually mortify this old body that we may finally receive a new body not so full of sin nor so inclined to all manner of evil as the life we now live. Give us bodies that will not become sick, nor suffer persecutions, nor die. Give us bodies redeemed from all temporal and spiritual misery, like your own glorified body, dear Lord Jesus Christ. Grant that the glad and blessed day of our redemption and glorification may come soon, and that we may realize it as we now hear and believe your word. Amen.

183.

For Preparation to Await Christ's Coming with Joy

Dear Lord, awaken us that we may be prepared to receive your Son with joy when he comes and to serve him with a pure heart. Graciously hurry the coming of that day. Bless and prepare us with wisdom and strength that in the meantime we may walk wisely and uprightly. May we joyfully wait for the coming of your dear Son and so depart blessed from this valley of sorrow. Amen.

184.

For Restoration of What the Devil Has Attempted to Destroy

Dear Lord Jesus Christ, the gospel is suffering. Your name is profaned. Christians are persecuted and murdered. The right doctrine is suppressed. The devil's rule of wickedness is spreading. All the blessed departed Christians and saints who lie forgotten in the earth have returned to dust and ashes. Come and display your glory in your church. Restore your name and the blood of martyrs, and bring them again to their glory. Amen.

185.

For an End of All Misery

O Lord Jesus Christ, will not this misery finally come to an end, and the glory of the children of God soon begin? You have promised us the day when you will free us from every kind of evil. If it be your will, let it come even in this hour right now, and end all misery. Amen.

INDEX A

Luther prefaces every part of the Small Catechism with the words: In the plain form in which it is to be taught by the head of a family. According to this instruction the Small Catechism may be profitably used in connection with Luther's prayers as a guide to family worship. Luther prayed until he had the catechism, and then he studied and prayed the catechism every day as long as he lived. Thus the underlying spiritual meaning of the catechism can be more easily fathomed by Luther's prayers and instruction for prayer than by the very best of the countless books that have been written on it.

Catechism

While studying and meditating on

The First Commandment 50-51
The Second Commandment 51-52
The Third Commandment 52-53
The Fourth Commandment 53-55
The Fifth Commandment 55-56
The Sixth Commandment 56-57
The Seventh Commandment 58
The Eighth Commandment 58-59
The Ninth and Tenth Commandments 59-60
For obedience to the Commandments 83
The First Petition 28-29, 43-44
The Second Petition 29-31, 44
The Third Petition 31-32, 45
The Fourth Petition 33-35, 45-46
The Fifth Petition 35-36, 46-47
The Sixth Petition 36-37, 47
The Seventh Petition 38, 47-48
Amen 48
The entire Lord's Prayer 43
The First Article of the Creed 60-61
The Second Article of the Creed 61-62
The Third Article of the Creed 62

INDEX B

Home and Family

For God's guidance in finding a devout husband or wife 93
For help to meet parental responsibilities 94
For help with responsibilities 86
Requesting God to be head of the family 94
For preservation of home and property 34
Entrusting a child to God 94
Commending all to the Lord 98
The Lord can and will provide for the body 97
I shall not want 97
For blessings and protection 95
For the best use of our means 96
A dying father commends his family to God 105
Prayer of a servant 95